About the editor:

MATHEW AHMANN served as Executive
Secretary of the National Conference on
Religion and Race. It was his initiative
which brought the meeting into being.
Mr. Ahmann is the Executive Director
of the National Catholic Conference for
Interracial Justice, and is the editor of
The New Negro (1961). He makes his
home in the Hyde Park section of
Chicago with his wife and four children.

............RACE:

Challenge to Religion

RACE:

CHALLENGE TO RELIGION

Original Essays and *An Appeal to the Conscience* from the National Conference on Religion and Race

Edited by

MATHEW AHMANN

HENRY REGNERY COMPANY
CHICAGO
1 9 6 3

The essays in this volume are based on papers delivered at the National Conference on Religion and Race, convened by the Department of Racial and Cultural Relations of the National Council of Churches, the Social Action Commission of the Synagogue Council of America, and the Social Action Department of the National Catholic Welfare Conference. *An Appeal to the Conscience of the American People* was unanimously adopted at the close of the Conference by the delegates of 70 participating organizations. The Conference was held at the Edgewater Beach Hotel in Chicago from January 14 to January 17, 1963.

Preparation for the Conference was assisted by grants from: The Acquinas Fund, the Joseph P. Kennedy, Jr., Foundation, the William J. Kerby Foundation, the Irwin Sweeney Miller Foundation, and the Rockefeller Brothers Fund.

Mathew Ahmann, editor of the volume, served as Conference Executive Secretary. He is the Executive Director of the National Catholic Conference for Interracial Justice.

© 1963 by Henry Regnery Company
Chicago 4, Illinois
Manufactured in the United States of America
Library of Congress Catalog Card No. 63-13762

PREFACE

The National Conference on Religion and Race represents, for the first time in the United States, the formal cooperation of our major faith bodies on a common moral and social problem. The Conference was convened by agencies of the National Council of Churches, the Synagogue Council of America, and the National Catholic Welfare Conference. Sixty-seven additional religious and religiously identified groups participated in the meeting by selecting delegates to attend. Several other national religious bodies sent observer delegates to take part in the deliberations.

The meeting was conceived as a distinctively religious commemoration of the centennial of the Emancipation Proclamation made effective by President Abraham Lincoln in January, 1863. The Conveners hoped and planned for a Conference which would concretely examine the role of religious institutions in race relations, and then move on to propose and inspire renewed action, and interreligious projects to increase the leadership of religion in ending racial discrimination in the United States.

The essays in this book, by their number and length, may tend to hide the fact that the delegates present felt the theme of the meeting was action. The talks provided a setting for the real heart of the meeting—32 workgroups in which lay and

clerical religious leaders from all over the United States re-
viewed concrete problems facing religion and religious institutions in race relations.

Workgroups dealt with concrete matters: racial exclusion in
congregations and denominations; programs to educate members on moral issues in race relations; use of national and local
policy and programs in the desegregation of religious institutions; the responsibility of religious institutions as employers;
the responsibility of the church and synagogue as administrators; educational resources of religious institutions; the role of
church and synagogue in urban and suburban neighborhoods,
and in rural areas.

Groups of delegates also dealt with the relation of religious
institutions to voluntary civic groups and movements, as religious people worked for desegregation and racial integration.
Others were concerned with the relationship between religious
groups working for interracial justice, and the relation of religious groups working for interracial justice to governmental
and political forces.

In each of these groups, delegates first made a candid ap-
praisal of the weaknesses and strengths of religious work for
race relations. They dwelt on the racial abuses still extant within
the life of religion itself. Then they moved on to propose ideas
and map programs to correct racial abuses within religious institutions, and to quicken the impact of organized religion on
United States racial patterns.

Some sixty-two practical program suggestions were accepted
in a closing plenary session. While delegates, chosen by their
groups, could not commit their groups, there was firm resolve
to use the proposed program ideas within national religious
groups, as well as in local communities around the country.

Indeed, the weeks prior to the meeting saw initial steps taken
in ten local communities around the country to organize top

flight interreligious committees which would implement Conference findings by developing interreligious action programs. And the weeks immediately after the Conference saw spontaneous developments along these lines take place in a number of cities and states.

The Conference Steering Committee and the delegates were conscious of the need to extend the influence of the meeting, and so provided for the maintenance of a national interim secretariat. This secretariat and a continuing Steering Committee also have responsibility for publishing Conference findings not contained in this book, for evaluating accomplishments of the meeting, and for proposing further joint program ideas to the participating groups. While the decision taken at the meeting indicated the secretariat should continue for a period of only four to seven months, delegates felt strongly that interreligious action for interracial justice must go on, increase in its impact on our divisive racial patterns, and especially develop specific local projects in our many urban and rural areas.

Secretariat responsibilities are being transferred to a strengthened Steering Committee, and the United Church of Christ has released Dr. Galen R. Weaver to serve as interim Executive Secretary.

To the 657 delegates present in Chicago from January 14-17, 1963, there was no doubt that the work of the National Conference on Religion and Race only began when the meeting itself ended.

While interracial justice was the goal which has called forth this demonstration of religious unity, an underlying concern was the relationship between religion and society. How do religious values influence and shape our society? How do religious institutions behave if they want their values to produce constructive social change?

While acknowledging some notable religious accomplishments in race relations—not the least the religiously motivated non-violent-movement inspired by Dr. Martin Luther King, Jr.—conferees acknowledged the collective guilt of the religious bodies in America; guilt for malpractice which contributed to the climate which produced the Civil War; guilt for the racial abuses still found in religious bodies; and even more, they acknowledged the massive fear of positive action to open our society so that every man is accepted by every other man.

There was a note of frustration and almost desperation which kept cropping up in deliberations. But there was no despair. The meeting was a solid demonstration of the eagerness of religious men and women to break unnecessary social and institutional restraints and give real leadership in resolving the great dilemma of America's conscience.

Three main lines of action seemed to emerge in the thought of delegates.

1. The conscience of each individual communicant of a religious group must be informed. Definitive policies of moral education on racial justice and love must be adopted and administered in all religious bodies. They must affect seminary education, the intraining education of clerical and lay leaders, adults from pulpits, and children. This education must be conducted in terms so concrete that the conscience is disturbed, so that any man can see that toleration of racial segregation in his neighborhood, his worklife, and the life of his religious body makes his faith irrelevant. As Dr. Heschel says in his paper, the man who permits racial segregation, really segregates God. Man must also see that religious values will not even permit him to segregate racially in his private social life. No part of the life of the people of God is apart from His judgment. In the far reaching meaning of religious commitment, religion does go much further and makes greater demands than government or other social institutions can ever make. Religion is not a crea-

tion of man, but of God, and adherents to our Jewish and Christian traditions must fulfill the command of God to draw *no* artificial line between man and man. The theme of the Conference was: "Challenge to Justice and *Love*."

2. Religious institutions must correct their own abuses. Again specific policies eliminating racial segregation in the life of religious and religiously administered institutions must be adopted and administered in all religious bodies. A religious body which preaches a doctrine of the oneness of humanity, the equality of all men created by God, denies its nature if it does not scrupulously root out those sore spots in its own institutions which divide brother from brother, and conscience from God.

Delegates to the Conference were not naive. They might hope for, but did not expect a rapid fire development in religious bodies which have been slow to respond to the moral challenge our racial patterns have placed before them. But they did pledge to see to the constant development of policy and administration which would enable religious institutions to cleanse themselves of their own sins, and be free to give leadership to a confused country.

3. Finally delegates were concerned with the specific relation between religious institutions, as social institutions, and our society. The life of a synagogue or a church in a local community shapes the response of that community to interracial challenge. Religious groups can refuse to contract or purchase from concerns which have not taken deliberate steps to eliminate racial discrimination in employment policies. Religious groups do manage social and welfare institutions which can respond to the needs of people caught in the misery of the slum ghetto. Religious groups together can conduct the kind of demonstrations which will awaken the conscience of Americans. Religious groups together can give forceful testimony before governmental and civic bodies. Indeed, delegates shared a posi-

tive belief that joint religious action in our communities was the one force which could dramatically alter racial patterns, bring racial justice with rapidity, free the conscience of white people from a burden of guilt, and shape the kind of social patterns which would enable all men to contribute their talents to the development of our world.

There was, then, a conviction present in the Conference that religion should influence our society not only through the informed communicant, who acts on religious principle, but also through the proper exercise of institutional power. Religious groups bear institutional responsibility, too. As Rabbi Adler says in his essay, religious bodies have every right to behave as other social institutions in contributing to the life of our society.

It was with these convictions, I believe, that the delegates to the National Conference on Religion and Race left the meeting hall, to work with renewed vigor for a just and open society.

It was my good fortune to be deeply involved in planning and preparing for this historic Conference. It was a pleasure for me because of the task before it, and also because of the many people who gave of themselves so deeply, and in such a splendid demonstration of interreligious cooperation to make the meeting a good one. It is never possible to acknowledge the contributions everyone made, but if the meeting is productive of new vigor in religious work in race relations the help of the following must be recognized.

The Rev. Gene Wesley Marshall was released temporarily from the staff of the Ecumenical Institute of the Church Federation of Greater Chicago. He joined my staff at the National Catholic Conference for Interracial Justice, and brought unique talents for administering the many details of a meeting like this, and for inspiring others to make their best contributions.

Conference direction was given especially by the following

representatives of the convening agencies: Dr. J. Oscar Lee of the Department of Racial and Cultural Relations, National Council of Churches; Rabbi Philip Hiat, Executive Vice-President of the Synagogue Council of America; and the Rev. John F. Cronin, S.S., Assistant Director of the Social Action Department, National Catholic Welfare Conference.

I wish also to thank the Conference Chairman Dr. Benjamin E. Mays, and the Committee Chairmen, Rabbi Marc H. Tanenbaum who was helpful from the inception of the Conference, Mr. Fletcher Coates for his public relations services, Miss Thelma Stevens, Dr. Garry Oniki, Rabbi Balfour Brickner, the Very Rev. Msgr. Daniel M. Cantwell, the Rev. Arthur E. Walmsley, Mr. John McDermott, Dr. Edgar Chandler, Rabbi Irving Rosenbaum, and the Honorable James B. Parsons.

Mr. Donald Graham, Vice Chairman of the Continental Illinois National Bank and Trust Company, and Mr. Irving J. Fain, Chairman of the Commission on Social Action of Reform Judaism provided generous leadership in raising necessary funds.

And I am personally indebted to Dr. Nathan Lander and Miss Peggy Roach.

MATHEW AHMANN
February 2, 1963

CONTENTS

xiv   Contents

INTRODUCTION

Dr. Benjamin E. Mays

Chairman, National Conference on Religion and Race
President, Morehouse College, Atlanta, Georgia

On January the first, 1863, two significant meetings were held in Boston, Massachusetts. The people assembled that day to rejoice and to thank God for the signing of the Emancipation Proclamation by Abraham Lincoln, thus ending 244 years of physical slavery which had been in operation since 1619.

The first meeting was held in Music Hall, Boston. If you had been living on the afternoon of January 1, 1863, and if you had been present in Music Hall, you would have seen some of the great literary figures celebrating and rejoicing as if they themselves had just been emancipated from bondage. Who were some of them?

You would have seen Henry Wadsworth Longfellow, Oliver Wendell Holmes, Charles Eliott Norton, John Greenleaf Whittier, Edward Everett Hale, Francis Parkman, and Ralph Waldo Emerson. And last, but by no means the least, Harriett Beecher Stowe. Charles Sumner was absent because his invitation arrived too late. Wendell Phillips had a previous commitment.

Emerson opened the meeting with the reading of a Boston

1

hymn which he had completed that morning. Here is one of the stanzas:

> I break your bonds and masterships,
> And I unchain the slave.
> Free be his heart and hand henceforth
> As mind and wandering wave.

Emerson was followed by music, highlighted by Beethoven's Fifth Symphony, with Carl Zerrahn conducting the Philharmonic Orchestra.

Harriet Beecher Stowe, sitting inconspicuously in the balcony, was called upon to speak. She walked slowly down the rail of the balcony—so deeply moved that she could only weep and bow.

The counterpart to this meeting was an evening assembly in Tremont Temple, Boston. Though sponsored by a predominantly Negro group, it was an integrated audience. Commenting on this meeting Frederick Douglass said: "We were not all of one color but we all seemed to be one color that day." Another Negro speaker, John S. Rock, commented that this was a great day for his country and for his race.

Why did they celebrate? Hale, Parkham, Longfellow, Whittier, Emerson, Stowe, Douglass and Rock? They celebrated because to them the emancipation of the slaves was not a military necessity, not a political gesture, not a diplomatic move— emancipation was a moral necessity. To them slavery was immoral, a cancer destroying the soul of religion and democracy, just as real cancer destroys the body. That's why they celebrated. They rejoiced that Lincoln had issued and signed the Emancipation Proclamation.

Why do we come one hundred years after Lincoln? Catholics, Jews and Protestants? We come because we too believe that racial discrimination and prejudice are immoral and cancerous and that they destroy the very vitals of democracy and religion, and undermine the foundation of both church and state.

We come because we stand on a solid doctrinal foundation. We affirm together that God is the ground of our existence, Creator, Sustainer, Judge. We hold that God is Father of *all* mankind, and that all men are brothers under God. We hold together that man is made in the image of God and that the life of each and every person is of intrinsic worth and value. This common doctrine cuts across all boundaries—national, religious, racial, class and caste. It is a common platform upon which Jews, Catholics and Protestants *all* stand. In believing this, we know that this doctrine must apply to each and every person everywhere, or it applies to none. God is the Creator of all mankind or He is the Creator of no part of it. He is the Father of all or He is the Father of none. The life of every person is sacred or the life of no person is sacred. If God cares for the greatest, He cares for the least. Either all or none. In this belief, Jews, Catholics and Protestants unite. We come because "We hold these truths to be self evident that all men are created equal, that they are endowed by their Creator with certain unalienable rights, that among these are life, liberty and the pursuit of happiness, That to secure these rights, Governments are instituted among men deriving their just powers from the consent of the governed." We believe then that life, liberty and the right to pursue happiness are gifts of God and not governments. It is the function of government to protect life, liberty, and one's right to pursue happiness. Although this document was pronounced when slavery was an accepted institution, the Declaration of Independence must apply to all or none.

We are here this week because we feel that the time has come for the three major faiths to speak to the nation with a united voice on what is one of the most crucial problems confronting mankind today. In questions of ethics and morals, we believe that religion should lead and not follow. It may be that if religion had taken the leadership, emancipation might have come without a Civil War and without the hatred that the War engendered. It may be that if the Church and Synagogue had led the way in desegregating their congregations, the May 17, 1954 decision of the United States Supreme Court might have been unnecessary. The so-called secular society would have followed the leadership of the Church and Synagogue.

The signing of the Emancipation Proclamation and the enacting of the 13th, 14th, and 15th Amendments brought physical freedom to the newly emancipated people. But the struggle to emancipate the mind and free mankind from prejudice and discrimination had to be left to those who followed Lincoln.

We come this week to think together, to work together, to pray together and to dedicate ourselves to the task of completing the job which Lincoln began 100 years ago.

We recognize the fact that we have had 100 years to make religion real in human relations and that we may not have another 100 years to make good on our theological commitment. We did not seek world leadership, but the Second World War thrust it upon the United States. The United States is the leader of the free world and it is the most powerful industrial nation in the annals of man. No nation in history has been so favorably circumstanced as the United States. But world leadership requires more than industrial and military might. It requires that we practice at home what we seek to sell to the world. So we are here because our consciences will not let us rest in peace until we implement, more fully, in deed what we expound in words. And as long as we say we believe in God, the brotherhood of man and in the Declaration of Independence, we have no choice but to strive with might and main to close the gap between theory and practice. Until we do this, we play a hypocritical role and wear an uneasy conscience.

We believe that this conference will create in us a new sense of urgency to do in the next ten years what we failed to do in the past 100 years—abolish from among us racial discrimination and prejudice. Other countries that repudiate God, deny the God given worth of the individual, and lay no claim to a Declaration of Independence, a Bill of Rights, and a 14th Amendment may hesitate and falter on this question, but the moral leadership of the world is in the hands of the United States of America. We dare not fail the world in this crucial moment of history!

We come because great responsibility rests on our shoulders. God has blessed America. No nation in history has achieved so much in so short a time. In less than two centuries we have become the wealthiest nation in history. Our standard of living is the highest in the world. Our military might is probably superior to that of any other nation. Our literacy is high. Never before has a country been in the enviable position where practically every nation on earth looked to if for some kind of aid. Whether they hate us or love us, the nations respect us and accept our aid and in many instances our leadership. Neither Rome nor England in its heyday carried the responsibility for world leadership as that which has fallen upon our shoulders.

This enviable position makes our country morally vulnerable. The Biblical injunction is applicable here. "To whom much is given of him much is required." Our greatness in other areas will amount to naught unless our moral leadership in human relations equals or surpasses our industrial and military power. Segregation in God's house, a few Little Rocks, Oxfords, New Orleans, Albanys do more to tear down our moral leadership in the world than our billions given in foreign aid can build up. These are not the main reasons why we must abolish racial discrimination and prejudice. We must abolish them because it is right so to do. But we can not dismiss the fact that the eyes of the world are upon us, and what we do in human relations speaks so loudly that the nations cannot hear what we say about religion and democracy.

We come today 100 years after Lincoln to seek ways and means of eliminating human injustices because we love the United States. It is my candid belief that if the United States so favored by God cannot implement its religious ideals in the area of race and culture, no other nation will or can. If men of all races cannot live together in mutual respect and helpfulness in the United States, religion and democracy as we know them will be doomed in the world.

In one sense, it may matter little what happens to minority groups in America—Negroes, Jews, Indians, Japanese, and Chinese. But it matters much what happens to the soul of America, to our democracy, and to our Judeo-Christian faith. If these lights go out, may God have mercy on our souls. If we cannot build the brotherhood of man in the United States I despair of its ever being built anywhere in the world. So we come today, Catholics, Jews, and Christians to confess our sins before God and dedicate ourselves anew to our religious ideals to the end that the emancipation which Lincoln began 100 years ago may become a reality in our time.

....

*The Inner Life of
Church and Synagogue
in Race Relations*

The Inner Life of Church and Synagogue in Race Relations

REV. WILL D. CAMPBELL

"Hear, O Israel: The Lord our God, the Lord is One."

The traditional Shema, as old as Israel itself, should be enough to solve the race problem.

It hasn't solved it.

The response which often follows certainly should have been enough to prevent the centuries of prejudice, discrimination and hate we have experienced: "Thine, O Lord, is the greatness, and the power, the glory, and the victory, and the majesty; for all that is in the heaven and in the earth is *Thine*; *Thine* is the Kingdom, O Lord, and *Thou* are exalted as head above all." There is really nothing one can say beyond that concerning the subject before us. What can we say after we have acknowledged the existence of God in the Shema? The only thing we can do is try to define what kind of God we have acknowledged and the response does it for us. It says He is the kind of God who has all power, all greatness, all glory, and the victory and the majesty. It says He is the kind of God to whom everything in heaven and on the earth belongs. It says He is the God who is exalted as head of everything. He alone is sovereign

9

and all our fates and destinies belong to Him. That should have been enough to know.

It wasn't.

Likewise since 1521 when the first Roman Catholic altar was erected in what is now the state of Florida, day after day, in parishes scattered from Minnesota to Alabama, from Cape Hatteras to San Francisco Bay the priest, just before the most important part of the Mass, namely the re-enactment of the Last Supper of Jesus, has turned to the people and said *Orates Fratres*. Pray *Brothers* . . . that my sacrifice and yours may be acceptable in the sight of God. You are brothers. Day after day after day *Orates Fratres*, no condition, no qualification, no exceptions, those two powerful words are spoken wherever and whenever the Mass is celebrated. Whether in Lewiston, Maine or Biloxi, Mississippi, the words are the same. And they are said, not in a general and nebulous way from a top level conference or council where there is always the hazard of their being lost between there and the living level but they, like the Shema, are said in a local situation, to a congregation gathered, to the family circle. Our subject is the inner life of church and synagogue. It is at this level that these words are spoken. They should have been enough to solve the problem of race in America.

They haven't solved it.

Again in Protestant Christianity Sunday after Sunday the people stand and affirm: "I believe in God the Father Almighty, Maker of heaven and earth." Or they stand and recite, "In *His* hand are all the corners of the earth; and the strength of the hills in His also. The sea is *His* and He made it; and His hands prepared the dry land." Or from the *Jubilate Deo*, "Be ye sure that the Lord He is God; it is He that hath made us, and not we ourselves; we are His people." This constant affirmation and reaffirmation of the absolute sovereignty of God, as

creator, redeemer and sustainer, should have been enough to
have shown us the total irrelevance of race, the frailty of man,
the folly of such Bible Belt absurdities as, "God was the original
segregationist."

These words, the Shema, the words from the Mass, the central message of most Protestant liturgy scream out at us that
life is suffering and sorrow, and the beginning of death, that we
all come forth like a flower and are cut down and are of a few
days and full of trouble, and all flesh is grass and we are all here
dying together. They alone should have been enough to teach
us the error of our ways in dividing people into such categories
as race.

But the truth is they haven't.

Some Jews who are active in the life of the synagogue continue to respond to the Shema by going out and joining the
White Citizens' Councils. Father J. H. Fichter, one of the
world's foremost authorities in the Sociology of Religion, found
in his study called *Southern Parish* (J. H. Fichter, Southern
Parish, Vol. I, the Dynamics of a City Church, Chicago, 1951)
that Catholic parishioners may indeed hear the words of the
Mass daily but often take it to mean that they are brothers at
the altar rail at prayer but not on the street car or in the school
room. And Protestants have continued to number among them
more racists than perhaps any other religious group in the
world. This despite their avowed belief in a God Who became
man to die that all men may be drawn into one family—the
Church. This despite the Beatitudes which most Protestant
Christians know by rote before they can read. Blessed are the
meek, blessed are the merciful, blessed are the pure in heart,
blessed are the peacemakers. Where is there mercy, where is
meekness, where is there purity of heart, where is there peace-
making in racist doctrine, a doctrine which yet rules on the
throne in every segment of American life, in every industry, in

every region, in every mass medium, in every profession?

Despite the Decalogue, despite the Mystical Body, despite the strong emphasis on the absolute Sovereignty of God, despite the Beatitudes, every religion represented here today is deeply afflicted with the cancerous cells of racism.

So perhaps it is ludicrous that we should be here talking about the inner life of church and synagogue. Perhaps the Black Muslims and the White Citizens' Councils are right. Perhaps it has now come down to a matter of sheer naked survival and that we should now take our stand, not on the basis of our religious faith and heritage, but on the basis of the color of our skin.

Or perhaps we are already irrelevant. Perhaps if we are not ludicrous in our presence then maybe it is sheer madness. There is a scene in a novel of some years ago which strikes me as being tragically descriptive of church and synagogue in the American racial crisis. The scene takes place on the sky balcony of a large hotel. The symbolism is too obvious to miss. A band is playing and people are dancing and making merry. At a table are four people playing bridge. One of the men is dealt a dummy hand. He places it upon the table, walks over to the balcony rail and looks far down to the street below him. Drifting lazily out of the basement window, a tiny wimper of smoke can be seen. He lights a cigarette and when he has finished it, crushes it upon the floor, walks into the dancing couples and dances with a beautiful girl. He returns to the table and during the course of the game he is again dealt a dummy hand. Again he goes to the balcony rail, lights a cigarette and gazes downward. This time he sees flames lashing their tongues out the fifth story window. He calmly finishes his cigarette, walks out onto the the dance floor, dances with the beautiful girl and once more returns to the bridge table where in a little while he is dealt another dummy hand. Again he walks quietly over to the balcony rail and starts to light his cigarette. But this time the flames are leaping and stepping their deadly dance across his face, singeing brow and lashes as they move. And at this moment there is a crash at the door, the fireman breaking the door down with the shout, which is the central theme of the book, "Gentlemen, are you mad!"

This, it seems to me, essentially has been the history of the religious forces during the long, dark night of American racism.

We looked over the balcony from the comfort and security of a promising and prosperous young country and saw just a hint of smoke when good, sincere and conscientious business men began paying African tribesmen to capture and deliver their brothers into white hands. But for the most part we turned and walked away because, after all, had not the Apostle Paul admonished Onesimus to return to his master, Philemon?

We saw the curling smoke of slavery flowing from the fifth story window but turned and sat down, for in reality this was one way of converting the heathen and, really and after all, weren't they more happy singing in their shanty under the protective eye of Colonel Sartoris and the big house than they were in disease-ridden jungles?

We walked to the balcony and saw the billowy flames of secession and Civil War soaring over our heads and almost engulfing us. And Dr. James Silver, in his book, *Confederate Morale and Church Propaganda*, has shown that there was not one known clergyman of any faith opposing slavery in the South by the time the first shot was fired (though some had earlier) and that the war would have collapsed from lack of public sentiment and support had it not been for the morale supplied by the churches.

We witnessed that C. Van Woodward has called "the strange career of Jim Crow" rise to manhood and for the most part saw our role in it all as establishing departments of Negro work, floating little schoolhouses down rivers to educate Negro children and otherwise fitting into the segregated pattern . . . the flame, leaping over the banister and all around us and we were all set to take our place again at the bridge table when out of the darkness, knocking us into a state of consciousness on May 17, 1954, those nine old men with a shout, "Gentlemen, are you mad!" Your house is burning down, why did we have to tell you! Why the Court? Did not the prophets tell you? Did not the God of Abraham, Isaac and Jacob warn you? Is this not a moral and spiritual problem? Has it not to do with God and love and people and brothers and children of one God? "Gentlemen, are you mad!"

And no longer can we take our seat. No longer the casual smoking of a cigarette and the unconcerned dance with the beautiful girl. For nothing has slept since. All is motion, and the question must be answered. Are we indeed mad?

If our being here is not ludicrous, if it is not madness, then maybe it is too late for us to be here at all. Perhaps God has already moved out of our houses erected in His name and that such inner life as we may now know is but the growth of a man's beard after he has been placed in the casket. Professor W. W. Stout in a recent review reminds us of the time in the fifth century B.C. when the keepers of the oracle at Delphi had to admit the real presence of Apollo was not consistently with them. "However," he says, "they hoped for the best and kept the shrine open for declining business another eight hundred years." If would be presumptuous and possibly a sacrilege for me to maintain with any degree of certainty that this is happening today. But if God be God He can move in whatever circles He chooses.

And I do say that it is too late for us to be here. That is, it is too late now for us to establish harmonious relationships between the races on a worldwide scale. We who live in America are not inclined to take this seriously for Negro leadership in the field of civil rights had a fortunate beginning in America in the rise and development of the NAACP, and most organizations concerned with Negro rights which have come into being, in more recent years have, for the most part, been sophisticated and non-violent in orientation. However, a new phenomenon which we must face honestly is in America. The fact that it might be too late is irrelevant to our task. The fact that Cain might become Abel and Abel, Cain, that history might see a reversal of majority and minority positions cannot be our concern.

If it is indeed too late for us to be here then why *are* we here?

We are here as a religious people. We are Jews and Christians. We come from various theological and ecclesiastical backgrounds. There are things which we hold in common but I think it would be a mistake if this conference takes its stand on the symbol of three faiths meeting together. There are many things upon which we do not agree. But there seems little point in discussing that upon which we do or do not agree. Suffice it to say that we are here as a religious people. We are not here as civil libertarians first or as scientists or historians or lawyers, although some of us are all those things. We are gathered here because we are a religious people. Centennial Conference on Religion and Race is our title. We are here as Jews and we are here as Christians. Thus I would say that we are here to discuss the subject which has been given to us but maybe not in the order it reads. We, at least I, am not here to discuss how we can use the inner life of the church to solve the race question. This presupposes that there *is* a well defined and established inner life as a tool to be used. That this is not the case is rather widely accepted by students of the sociology of religion. Conor Ward in *Priest and People*, a book in a current English social research series says of St. Catherine Parish: "It could be said perhaps that the system of ecclesiastical organization . . . arose in the somewhat different circumstances of the . . . end of the nineteenth century and that in some respects it had not as yet adapted itself sufficiently to the new conditions and to a changed situation in the mid-twentieth century." I have little reason to doubt that what this scholar said of one Catholic parish in England is likewise true of most churches and synagogues on a local level in America.

If we are saying that there does not now exist sufficient inner life within local parishes to substantially influence social change we are still stuck with the question of why we are here.

I would like to suggest that instead of seeking a solution to the race problem through the inner life of church and synagogue it would be more realistic to seek a true inner life for church and synagogue *through* the race problem. For here is an issue that is virtually absolute. Unlike any other social problem religion has ever had to come to grips with, here is one on which there is no room for argument. Here is an issue which should never have been an issue in the life of church and synagogue for it was settled for the Jews in the wilderness when they were admonished to accept the Ger, the so-journer, the stranger within their gates; when God approved the marriage of Moses to an Ethiopian woman to the extent of giving Miriam leprosy for disapproving; and it was settled for Christendom at Pentecost when members of every race and nation and tongue were "altogether, in one place [integrated] hearing the mighty works of God."

Yet not only did what was so basic and elementary in our body of doctrine become an issue; it stands today as the most crucial issue in the life of both church and society. That something so elementary did become an issue can only lead us to the conclusion that something went wrong in the life of institutionalized religion—that if we had had that basic element, race would not have become a problem but that since it did our greatest hope is to recover that basic element.

What is the basic element? I would not wander to the brink of absurdity by trying to summarize each of the three faiths represented here today. I would say that where there exists a true understanding and acceptance of what we are as members of St. Mary's Church, or as members of Congregation Beth-El or members of First Methodist there does not exist a problem of race in that grouping because it is recognized that as a people of God the concept of race is neither tolerated nor recognized. *There* exists an inner life of a people of God.

If the basic theological assumptions of all faiths represented here do not tolerate the concept of race then how did it happen that race is such an issue in the life of religious communities? How and why did it happen?

I would like to suggest that it happened because the South won the Civil War. The Civil War was fought over the issue of race. One of the best historians on the Civil War period, Dr. James Silver, says it was this and nothing more. After all has been said about the economics and politics of it all, it was really a war of the abolitionist and the non-abolitionist. And it has been the racial theory of the non-abolitionist which has endured and is to be found in every area of American life.

And where in America, a democracy—a political system of equality—where in America, a nation of Jews and Christians, two religions refuting racism from the beginning, came this influence? For the answer I would turn to an article by the novelist, Walker Percy, published by *The Commonweal* a number of years ago. He says that while the South did live in a Christian edifice, it lived there in the strange fashion Chesterton spoke of, that of a man who will neither go inside nor put it entirely behind him but stand forever grumbling on the porch. And from that vantage point, infers Percy, he developed a religion which was neither Jewish nor Christian, but Greek. It seemed to have a theology of the Judeo-Christian tradition —at least in words and liturgy—but an ethic (that pattern of behavior resulting from any theological system) which was Stoic. The *noblesse oblige* of Southern aristocracy has often been condemned and the notion that he was "the best friend the Negro had" has been dismissed as a myth. It was not a myth. There was this period when he fought the Klan and defended the rights of his Negro charge. There was this bond which Faulkner describes between the Colonel Sartoris "who made himself responsible for his helpless 'freedom,' and the Lucas Beauchamps who accepted his leadership," and between them formed an alliance which worked for a long time. But it was an alliance based on the Stoic notion that sovereignty and the power and authority to rule inheres naturally in the best man. As Percy said, this nobility, and nobility it was—make no mistake about that—"was the nobility of the natural perfection of the Stoics, the stern inner summon to man's full estate, to duty, to honor, to generosity toward his fellowmen and above all to his inferiors—not because they were made in the image of God and were therefore lovable in themselves, but because to do them an injustice would be to defile the inner fortress which was oneself." The Southerner fought the Civil War, convinced that this power had inhered naturally in him and he outfoxed those who, following the war, occupied his land, convinced that he above all was prepared to do the decent and honorable thing toward the freedmen. And on the basis of the Stoic understanding of power and nobility and decency he did the best he could. But when his charges lost their manners, when Lucas Beauchamps quit coming to Colonel Sartoris, but

instead joined the NAACP and the labor union and turned to
the Federal Court and the Executive, and instead of asking, informed: "We are going to ride, we are going to vote, we are
going to go to school and we are going to eat in dignity and you
are going to help us," the Stoic understanding of man could not
survive the test. For in that concept, based on an hierarchical
structure, when one becomes insolent, when he demands instead of asking, when he refuses the *oblige* and the *noblesse*, the
Stoic no longer has a responsibility toward him. The following
paragraph of Percy's seems to sum up the point.

> For the Stoic there is no real hope. His finest hour is to sit
> tight-lipped and ironic while the world comes crashing
> down around him. It must be otherwise with the Christian.
> The urban plebs is not the mass which is to be abandoned to
> its own barbaric devices, but the lump to be leavened. . . .
> The Stoic has no use for the clamoring minority; the Chris-
> tian must have every use for it.

The White Citizens' Council member and the Neighborhood Protective Association member is right when he says the
rising mass has nothing to offer his former kingdom. Much of
the data he has about the behavior of the rising mass is accurate
though it does not take into account sociological reasons for
that behavior. But there is no point in challenging him on that
level and on that basis. As a Stoic he is right. As a Christian and
as a Jew he is wrong, bad wrong, dead wrong, heretically wrong,
for his data is irrelevant to the heritage he claims.

So what we are saying is that the greatest contribution the
local religious unit can make is to seek and to find, nay, to be
found of that inner life without which it is sounding brass and
tinkling symbols, without which it is nothing. Their greatest
contribution is to preach and proclaim and live their own particular and peculiar message, that which they and they alone

have. Unless we can say, "We are not pagans, this is the way we behave because we are in this household of faith, this is what it means to be a Jew, this is what is means to be a Christian, this is how we behave because of what we believe." Unless this can be said then I am convinced that all our techniques, all our gimmicks, program kits and human engineering will fail. And so will this conference fail unless it results in rediscovery and renewal of the hundreds of religious communities represented here.

There is strong racial consciousness and loyalty in every part of America and the new Executive order on housing may well dramatize the degree of hostility that exists in other regions as the court decision on education in 1954 did in the South. So the issue over which the Civil War was fought was not resolved and its body lies mouldering in the grave much less than John Brown's.

Still the question comes, what can we *do?* Although I insist that a more appropriate question is, "What can we be?" the question deserves treatment. But any treatment I give the question presupposes true renewal of church and synagogue in their inner life. Until we are able to proclaim categorically and with authority, "We are Jews and this is the way we behave in this household of God," and, "We are Christians and this is the way this family behaves because of what it is." Until we are able to say that—there is nothing we can do, for we are too much a part of the culture in which we live.

And I would say further that generally someone who has to ask doesn't really want to know. Often what we really mean is, "What can we do to improve race relations and still maintain the strength and rate of growth of the institution?" The answer to that question is, "Nothing!" For the cobblestones of a daring and radical and prophetic religion is the road to death. Furthermore, even if we ask the question in all sincerity with a well-defined and established inner life we must understand that the secular agencies and government are better prepared to do most of it than we are. We must understand that our actions must be based, not on what we may be able to accomplish, but on the basis of what we are, and on the basis of our very nature.

And the first thing we can do is repent. There can be no reconciliation without repentance. And we are all involved. You don't have to own a cotton plantation in Sunflower County, Mississippi, to be involved. If you wear a cotton shirt you contribute to American racism, you are a part of the sin we are discussing. Across the street from where I once had an office in an American city there was a house of prostitution—so they said. A small grocery located in the building was managed by a Negro lady. The establishment proper was owned by whites. We used to go there for take-out sandwiches when we had interracial gatherings and had to eat in the office. On one such occasion when I went for the sandwiches, the manager of the grocery was not there and in her place was the white proprietress. When I inquired as to where Mrs. X was, the white lady began to weep and told me of the untimely death of Mrs. X the night before. And then in fits of tears she told me of her deep affection for Mrs. X. And it was apparent that her tears were not the patronizing tears of the Old South weeping for a passed-on Aunt Jemima or a departed Mammy. Here was genuine grief for a friend and peer. This was in the era of the kneel-ins. And as I sought to console this proprietress of a house of prostitution, I could not help but feel the tragedy of a culture in which this woman would have been unwelcome in the respectable churches in the area, but was deeply mourned for in a bawdy house. No wonder a prophet whom most white council members and most neighborhood protective association members call Lord said to some of the "good" people of his day that those who sold their bodies for pay and those who cooperated with occupying forces for pay were closer to the Kingdom of which he spoke than they—"Truly I say to you, scalawags and whores enter the kingdom of God before you." Woe unto a generation when a human soul finds more acceptance and community in a whore house than in a church house!

Having repented what can a local congregation do—where can it go from there? Are we suggesting that the duty of the local congregation is to get together every weekend and say, "God is Supreme, let us pray"? Far from it. I would like briefly to outline nine areas where it seems to me a congregation which has discovered what it is as a people of God can work. I considered proposing ten but to use that number seemed presumptuous. Not all of them apply to all religions represented here.

Certainly high up on any list would be the area of housing. I am grateful that churches and religious groups have already pioneered in that field to some extent. Both the National Council of Churches and several denominational and religious groups have provided advisory services on a sustaining basis to local community organizations which have done such things as securing open occupancy pledges, gathering information and data on the private housing market, putting buyer in touch with seller and following up the situations in the capacity of counsellor as long as it is needed. These have been pilot projects. Now with the recent Executive Order on housing there will be a ready made opportunity in every American town and city for local congregations to carry out such a program. Any one of the convening agencies of this conference is prepared to offer materials which would give you the information needed. Whereas the school desegregation crisis has affected but a few southern communities, the housing order has more far-reaching implications and will offer every church and synagogue a chance not only to be the conscience of the community but also an opportunity to involve itself in appropriate direct action. It takes no genius to predict that the housing order, if enforced and supported, will do far more to change the racial picture in America than did the Supreme Court decision on public school education of 1954.

A second dramatic and significant development among minority groups is the current emphasis on voter education and registration. In some states nearly half the population is disfranchised on the grounds of race alone. Such agencies as the NAACP, CORE, the Southern Christian Leadership Conference, the Student Non-violent Coordinating Committee, and the Urban League are cooperating in voter education drives in a project administered by the Southern Regional Council. What more appropriate could a local congregation do than to sponsor one such drive itself working through its youth. It is disheartening to me that about the only time religion is mentioned in political circles is when the bigots inject it to discredit a candidate. Could it not become a major moral influence through such efforts as the one mentioned?

A number of previously all-white colleges and universities have now declared an open policy. But they are finding that no Negro students apply. Why could not a local congregation recruit and offer scholarships for students to attend these schools? Especially since most of the schools in that category are church related.

I would also mention a very interesting movement among some African Christians to send missionaries to America—not to preach racial tolerance, but to preach the gospel as they have understood it from other missionaries. If that movement develops the very act of their preaching to us, white America may

be spared. Local congregations can ask for such help just as
African congregations have requested it in the past. But it can't
be done in the old patronizing manner of thinking there is
something virtuous in seeing the cute and quaint African cos-
tumes on Sunday morning or during Brotherhood Week.
Rather we must ask because we need the freshness of their
preaching, because we need their witness and ministry for the
health of our souls.

There is a somewhat similar program which developed
among Seminary students in this country known as the Student
Interracial Ministry. These students give a summer to serve as
assistant pastor in a church where their race is not the dominant
one. White students serve as assistants in Negro congregations
and vice versa. A Southern Baptist congregation in North
Carolina had a Negro student pastor who for much of the
summer had full responsibility for all the work of the church.
Congregations in Georgia, Alabama, Mississippi, Texas, Tennessee, South Carolina and other states have also participated
in the program. Local churches throughout the country could
profit from such an experience. Or they could contribute funds
to that project so that others may participate.

There are silent sermons being preached throughout the
land by a group who call themselves "BROTHERS." Started
by a physically handicapped layman during the Little Rock
crisis, the group wears a little lapel pin and carries a small card
as a pledge that they will pray for the unity of mankind and
that they will work constantly for the disappearance of patterns
of separation and discrimination. They are not an organization,
they have no dues, no membership roles, no officers. I dare say
that all of you will see at least one such pin being worn at this
conference. Inquire as to its meaning.

Once a congregation has discovered its real nature it no

longer fears criticism or persecution and no longer needs to protect its institutional growth. It is then willing to be used up in the service of God and mankind. Thus it can then make use of the mass communications media to reach the community. Who, having a light, hides it under a bushel? Who? Why, churches and synagogues. When the going really gets rough if we venture out at all it is often after we have made sure the press won't be there and that no names will be named and no pictures made lest we ruin our *effectiveness*. Now we aren't really worried about our effectiveness are we? We're worried about our institutional hides. So for the most part we have turned radio and T.V. over to the bigots and crackpots who hawk their wares of bigotry in the name of religion on every band and channel in the country. When we have finally declared that we are a people of God and are against discrimination and injustices of all kinds we are no longer afraid to shout it to the winds. And he that hath ears to hear let him hear.

Or a local congregation can do what one let its leaders do in Oxford, Mississippi, on what the natives call "the longest night." Their priests went out into the face of death and hell as a sort of two-man truth squad, relieving students of knives, shovels, bottles, bricks and other more advanced trinkets of pleasure. What happened on that night made me proud to be a Mississippian for a few native sons, James Meredith one of them, Father Duncan Gray another, showed what it meant to be men of faith, and they are both products of Mississippi. Certainly I was ashamed of the chaff, but the grain stood out in a manner seldom witnessed in this century. And there is a subtle Oxford almost daily in the average American city. What's the difference really if two people are killed by bullets or two people die because they are forced to a life of squalor and poverty and ghettos and lack of opportunity because of the color of their skin. What difference except social respectability and headlines and subtleties. And it happens every day. But how many cities have a James Meredith to challenge it and how many local congregations provide or would even tolerate a Duncan Gray or a Kilmer Myers to "light the dark streets" in support of the challenge. This is not a defensive effort to say Mississippi isn't so bad after all. It is rather an effort to say it is worse than its most severe critics say but that it isn't different from the rest of America—it is typical. Take a neighborhood in Manhattan where 80% of the young people betweeen 16 and 18 years old who have finished high school or have dropped out and are Negroes and who find it utterly impossible to find employment and turn to all forms of death and despair—drug addiction, alcoholism, illegitimate relations, crimes of various sorts. Thousands are dying daily and their lives of crime are retreats from society and they suffer the same kind of denial—the denial of fellowship and opportunity—that James Meredith suffers. Consider the increasing breakdown of relationships between white liberals and Negro youths in these areas and it is frightening. When a congregation has found renewal, has found itself, it will not only lend its minister and laity to such a ministry, it will literally push them into it. The well have no need of a physician.

Or again Sunday Schools can get their studies out of cinder block classrooms painted a pretty blue and often as far from the world God placed us in as Oral Roberts is from the Mayo Clinic and the laboratory of human life; the human world of various racial and ethnic groups. Where is the community that does not offer a local church a peace corps situation, a children's camp to be built, a widow's house to be painted, a desecrated synagogue or a bombed church to be rebuilt? I would trade one weekend of such labor by an interracial group of young people who discuss with their leaders and experience with one another the dimensions of their faith, for a year's curriculum in the average Sunday School.

Well. I'm finished. We began by saying it is too late. It is never too late for faithfulness. In the process of our being faithful to the God we worship and seek to serve, society might be changed. But we must not be faithful in order to change society. And if there is to be any increase from the fruits of our labors, let God be the giver.

PART II

....

Religion and Race:
The Historical
Perspective

Religion and Race:
The Historical Perspective

Dr. Franklin H. Littell

In a recent interview, the legal advisory to Mr. James Meredith (Mr. Medgar Evers of the NAACP) commented that the
white ministers in Jackson, Mississippi, had failed to stand up
in the face of injustices and violence. "As far as speaking out,"
he said, "we don't know they exist."[1] Although in Oxford three
of the Protestant clergy showed exceptional moral courage in
dealing with the challenge to the Church's teaching,[2] the question will not down: Wherein is the captivity of the Protestant
churches, which has led to all too much silence of the American pulpits in the face of widespread triumph of violence and
anarchy?

Understanding the Nineteenth Century

To understand the special strengths and peculiar weaknesses
of the American churches, a brief glance at the course of religion in American history is necessary. There is a widespread
misapprehension that America has been, and still is, a "Christian nation," and therefore there is embarrassment and frustration among the sensitive when infidelity runs rampant. As a
matter of fact, the American people is but slowly being won

31

from heathenism to faithfulness, and the process is far from completed. The existence of racialism is one proof of that fact.

Contrary to the reactionary legend of the Nativists, the generation of the "Founding Fathers" was not the heyday of true religion and simple virtue—from which high level degenerate sons and daughters have been steadily falling away.[3] The legend is a white Protestant construct, and it is heart and core of the vicious assault of the Radical Right upon our present national leadership, and—more fundamentally—upon our Constitution and upon those agencies entrusted with interpreting and enforcing it. Since Catholics and even Jews sometimes seem appallingly vulnerable to the myth-making of the "Protestant underworld," one of the major contributions of Negroes to their fellow Americans may be to foster the suspicion that the "good old days" of Protestant hegemony, slavery, concubinage, limited suffrage, indentured servitude, religious persecution, and widespread illiteracy, were not so wonderful after all.

The truth is that the "Roundhead" coercion of the New England Way was unseemly and unsuccessful. And the "Cavalier" laxity of the southern colonial establishments was unlovely and fruitful of religious disaffection. With the collapse of the colonial state-churches, church membership fell to its true proportions—quite different from the inflated claims of establishments, then and now. The "Founding Fathers," being representative and responsible men, paid their church taxes. The generation of the "Founding Fathers" was a heathen generation, with no more than 7% holding church membership. The true history of American Protestantism has not been that of defending and preserving the pretensions of "Christendom," but of winning a whole people back to the churches on a voluntary basis. Today, nearly 70% are on church rolls and 96% of all Americans fourteen years of age and older claim to be affiliated.

Statistically, and in the practical expressions of the faith, the Golden Age of Protestantism in America lies not in antiquity but—potentially—directly ahead. The primitivist legend, so debasing to sound religion and corrupting to good citizenship, is a self-deception which must be struck down.

> I am waiting for my case to come up
> and I am waiting
> for a rebirth of wonder
> . . . .
> and I am waiting
> for the American Eagle
> to really spread its wings
> and straighten up and fly right
> . . . .
> I am waiting for the Second Coming
> . . . .
> I am waiting for the day
> That maketh all things clear
> . . . .
> and I am waiting
> for the deepest South
> to just stop Reconstructing itself
> in its own image.
> . . . .
> (Lawrence Ferlinghetti)[4]

The stance of looking backward ill-becomes citizens—whether Southerners or Northerners—of a country entrusted with the responsibility of self-realization and moral leadership on a world scale.

In point of fact, the shape of American Protestantism during the last century and a half has been given by mass evangelism. The representative churches on the scene have been the great revival churches—Baptist, Methodists, Disciples, and those off-shoots of Presbyterianism which abandoned orthodoxy for voluntaryism. Even the great social crusades, as Timothy L. Smith has demonstrated in an epochal study, were products of revivalism; the Social Gospel did not appear with the relaxation of intense faith and the sometimes emotional manifestations thereof, but as a result of "the zeal and compassion which the midcentury revivalists awakened for sinning and suffering men. And it rests in large measure upon social theories which they originated."[5] Not the maintenance of a legendary past, cast in the mold of European Christendom, but the proclamation of the "city which hath foundations, whose builder and·maker is God" (Hebr. 11:10), has graced American Protestant preaching at its best.

Foremost among the social crusades was the abolition of slavery. Beginning with Wesley during the Great Awakening, and carried right on down through Charles G. Finney and the Oberlin School, revivalism was identified with the anti-slavery cause. And the orthodox opponents of voluntaryism in religion were just as consistent in support of slavery. Robert J. Breckinridge, leader of the Old School during the Presbyterian Schism of 1837-38, said he was

> going to lay no burden on men which neither they nor their fathers were able to bear. . . . Never would he consent that it should be mooted at all, until the church had first got back upon sound and orthodox ground. . . .[6]

J. H. Thornwell, the most effective apologist for slavery in antebellum theological circles, was equally opposed to revivalism and what he called "the insane fury of philanthropy."[7] He also initiated a word association sequence which is still found in some disturbed groups today. "The parties in this conflict," he proclaimed, "are not merely abolitionists and slaveholders— they are atheists, socialists, communists, red republicans, jacobins, on the one side, and the friends of order and regulated freedom on the other."[8] By such inexorable logic (both past and present), unembarrassed by love and unhampered by humility, a system based on holding human beings as chattels may become "regulated freedom," mob violence may become an expression of "gracious living," and defiance of the American tradition of due process of law may be termed "a higher patriotism"!

Religious liberty, made workable by powerful appeals to voluntary acceptance of the religious obligation, was thus intimately related to the anti-slavery impulse. When revivalism found an economic basis in the free soil movement of the old Northwest, it became an irresistable force to emancipation.

Although slaveowners became increasingly resistant to evangelistic work among the slaves, the nineteenth century opened with both whites and Negroes in the little congregations of the awakened. It was the impending Civil War which, traumatic in so many areas of American life, fastened the pattern of racial segregation upon the Protestant churches.

But a second point about the revivals of religion is worthy of note: in meeting the problems of the newly freed, agencies and institutions created by the revivals were pre-eminent. Abraham Lincoln, perhaps the ablest American theologian of the nineteenth century, was in his religion a characteristic product of the camp meeting culture. So were Lincoln's generals— Clinton B. Fisk, Oliver Otis Howard, Samuel Chapman Armstrong, and others who left security of position and profession to work in the education of the freedmen. So was the American Missionary Association (AMA)—one of a long line of devoted efforts beginning with the American Board of Commissioners (ABCFM) in 1810 which owed their founding and subsequent support and staffing to the religious awakenings.

There is not enough space to more than note the astonishing growth of major colleges and universities and charitable institutions in the Negro community. At this juncture, the important point is that the growth of Negro church membership has kept pace with white membership during the Great Century of the expansion of Christianity. Indeeed, in spite of the most clever appeals, anti-Christian ideologies have found less following (percentage-wise) among the Negroes than among the whites. More than that, in the last half of the nineteenth century, when white churches north and south were often identifying uncritically with sectional interest and atmosphere, the Negro churches were rejoicing in the Year of Jubilee and praising the God of the nations and the generations.

Certainly the Church has had a greater formative role in the Negro community since World War II—the only war that has been important to Americans—than in the white community. For this we may all be profoundly grateful. What would our situation be in America today, facing our most important internal crisis, if the Negro leadership were at the level of Ross Barnett, Orville Faubus, Jimmy Davis, and Edwin Walker? Where would we be if the Negro community were as violent and undisciplined as many whites have shown themselves to be?

Americans Are "New Christians"

We have come upon one of the most critical issues of all: the tremendous statistical success of the churches during the nineteenth century was achieved by watering down the membership standards. The increase itself was one of the greatest in church history, and must be symbolized geometrically rather than arithmetically. The figures on successful home missions, which made the American churches the morning star of the "Younger Churches" and no longer an extension of European Christendom, run as follows:

$$
\begin{array}{ll}
1800 & 6.9\% \\
1850 & 15.5\% \\
1900 & 35.7\% \\
1926 & 50.2\% \\
1960 & 69.+\%[9]
\end{array}
$$

Around 1900, however, one large church after another formal-
ized the abandonment of church discipline. One result was
that several dozen smaller churches broke off from the major
bodies to reestablish some measure of internal integrity. Another result has been that the white churches are today virtually incapable of maintaining the most elementary internal
discipline to support fundamental theological and moral principles.

Most Americans in churches are first or second or at most
third-generation Christians. Racialism, which is the foremost
issue confronting the churches, has precisely the same relation
to our church life as polygamy in Africa or the bride-price in
Africa and Asia. That is, it is a typical case of the carrying over
into the Church of pre-baptismal practices which are contra-
dictory to Christian norms. This is a typical problem among
"new Christians," particularly in fields of extraordinary membership expansion, and can be viewed in many places and
periods of the past as well as in the present.

For example, when Christianity crossed the Rhine from
Gaul and in the 9th and 10th centuries hundreds of thousands
of tribesmen submitted in mass baptism, the "new Christians"
carried over into the Church their polygamy, their blood ven-
dettas, their trial by combat, their brutality toward the weak
and helpless. It took several generations of the most determined
instruction, salted by the sacrifices and martyrdoms of many
teachers, for the Church to consolidate the statistical gains into
something which could be called (roughly) "Christian." This
is precisely where we are, after a century and a half of mass
acquisitions, in American Protestantism. And I suggest we look
forward with hope rather than backward in despair.

There are those who refer to our era as "post-Christian."
Some come to this conclusion as romantic reactionaries, looking back to a "Christian America" which never existed except
in the formal sense. Others come to this conclusion because

they confuse the crisis in European Christendom with the situation in America, whereas the present identity of the latter is much more with the other areas of successful mission—with the younger churches of Africa, Asia, and the islands of the sea. Our American society is not "*post*-Christian;" it is, if anything, "*pre*-Christian."

Nevertheless, the Christians have been growing in clarity of mind on the matter of race.[10] Although the surreptitious propaganda of the "faceless" ones still circulates like a lingering virus in the bloodstream of our churches, and although some marginal sect-movements have attempted to cultivate popular support by attacking responsible churchmen, there has been no intellectually competent theological defense of racialism in America for generations. It is this which constitutes the fundamental difference between the situation in South Africa and in the USA.[11] As a matter of fact, the most sophisticated defense of racialism in recent decades has been made by anthropologists like Lathrop Stoddard[12] and Madison Grant.[13] American churches which practice racial discrimination do so with a bad conscience: they know that they are denying their own commitment to liberty, to missions, to Christian universalism.

The official positions of the churches are now plain enough, as can be seen by use of the appendix to the Campbell and Pettigrew volume on Little Rock.[14] It is in the maintenance of a standard of practice to conform to their verbalizations that they are weak. As Kyle Haselden has shown, other major church bodies have in the last generation joined the Congregationalists and northern Baptists with uncompromising statements, but "there is little evidence that the local white churches are yet taking seriously the resolutions and pronouncements of their respective official bodies."[15]

This brings us to the heart of the matter: where racialism today exists in the American Protestant churches it is a product of indiscipline. Racialism is a kind of heathenism, and its presence among the baptized is above all a sign of lack of discipline. For that matter, the general failure of the Protestant churches to maintain a standard of civic excellence among their members is of the same order and points to the same problem. The churches were clear in condemning anarchy, mob violence, and the law of the jungle, long before they achieved clarity on racialism; yet they have shown themselves unable as yet to restrain or discipline the most arrogant effrontery to the Lord of the Church and disgraceful disloyalty to American political institutions by mobs of untrained "new Christians."

Church Discipline

We do not need, in short, many more general resolutions in the field of religion and race. What we need is disciplined witness, backed by positions with binding quality. In dealing with this matter several Catholic prelates have shown more courage to date than any of the Protestant bodies. The Church is not a cave of all the winds of doctrine; neither is it an association of moral anarchists. Where salvation is involved—and nothing less is at stake on this front—the Church speaks and acts with integrity, or else it is not the Church of Jesus Christ at all. This, from a Christian point of view, is the basic question put by racialism.

In the political arena, race is not the basic issue: it is only the precipitation point of controversy. The real controversy concerns just government, government representative of every citizen sharing our common destiny. Are we to have republican forms of government such as guaranteed by the U.S. Constitution (Art. IV, Sec. 4, Par. 1)? Not long ago, a U.S. Senator gained notoriety by commenting that he had not found an African nation capable of self-government. The Senator missed the point. The world awaits with anticipation the future of young nations already capable of producing men like Chief Albert John Luthuli, Sir Francis Akame Ibraim, Julius Myrere, Leopold Senghor, John Karefa-Smart, Felix Houphouet-Boigny, Kenneth Kauanda. The problem over which the world agonizes, the particular problem of our country, is what to do with older states which can't come up with anything better than Mr. Ellender.

In the religious arena, race is not the basic issue: it is only the moment of truth which exposes our nakedness. An individual once stood on the floor of the most powerful legislative body in the world, the U.S. Senate, and launched into a violent and obscene attack on American citizens whom he called "kikes," "niggers," "dagoes," etc. When decent men rose to protest, he asserted defensively that he was "a good Christian," "a good Methodist." This prompted the former president of the National Council of Methodist Youth to write in *The Christian Century*:

> The Church ought to have sufficient ethical sensitiveness and power to reprimand or to remove from membership persons who ideas and actions are totally contrary to Christian standards. In some congregations people who drink, commit adultery, or are divorced suffer some penalties for their conduct. A more significant Christian ethic would be to somehow penalize men like Bilbo and Eastland and disavow the ideas which they expressed on the floor of the Senate. . . .[16]

In September of 1962 a faithful Christian shepherd attempted to restrain a mob leader and former military person who was bringing public disgrace on their church, on our country, on an old university. The mob leader turned on the pastor scornfully and proclaimed publicly that he was "ashamed to be an Episcopalian." Classical Christian practice, amply supported by Scripture and ecclesiastical law, would indicate how he could be relieved of that embarrassment! and the Church of Jesus Christ from the shame of public sin.

Foremost for the church is not racial justice or good citizenship, although both are important in the scales of history. The most important issue from a Christian point of view involves eternity itself: Are our churches truly the Church of Jesus Christ, the Prince of Peace?—of Him who gathers the peoples, and judges nations and generations?

Whatever our fellow citizens of other religions or philosophies may think of our churches, and they are free to join or to abstain in good faith, they will understand the statement that at the bar of judgment are the sincerity and integrity of our religious commitments. The enormous popularity of religion, or at least of religiosity, has been bought by eliminating standards of membership—both preparatory and full. As Rufus Jones once said, our churches have become so big they are like Robinson Crusoe's goat pasture: the fences are so distant and the fields are so big that the goats inside are as wild as the goats outside!

The most useful and relevant contribution the churches could make to racial justice would not be a political act at all: it would be to become truly the Church—disciplined as a community of witness, loving in service to the Least Brother, intercessory for the helpless and defenseless. Nothing could contribute more to the resolution of our diffiulties than for the Church to mean what she says—maintaining an internal service which would do honor to her universal Lord, enforcing a standard of order which would civilize and cultivate some of the untamed jungles of our social existence.

An early Father once explained how the Christians lived in anticipation of things to come: "Christians are better than the laws." Today, in many parts of the United States, the conduct of the Christians is worse than the laws.

Protestants and Catholics

This conference is unique for its sponsorship, and in binding the American people together, the fact that it represents Protestant-Catholic and Christian-Jewish cooperation is *almost* as important as the theme itself.

During the colonial period the shape of American religion was largely given by the Congregational and Anglican established churches. In the founding of the new nation the Presbyterians played a particularly significant role. At the time of the Declaration of Independence, out of 3.6 millions in the thirteen revolting colonies only c. 20,000 were Catholics and c. 6,000 were Jews. The rest were officially Protestant. The origins of 85% of the population lay in the British Isles.

During the nineteenth century, the shape of American religion was largely given by the revival churches—Methodists, Baptists, Disciples. The nineteenth century continuum of religious and cultural values ended in Europe with World War I, but it was not seriously undermined in the United States until World War II. In spite of the self-image, however, which served to perpetuate the notion that America was a Protestant nation and Christianity part of the common law of the land, the home missions which actually won the people back to the churches on a voluntary basis operated on more realistic principles: America was missionary territory, just as truly as India or China or West Africa. Protestantism in America, if the gains in membership, attendance, and support can be consolidated and standards of disciplined witness reestablished, has a far greater potential for good than ever in the state-church period.

At the same time the shift to voluntaryism was being accomplished in Protestantism of English background, the foundations were being laid for an America pluralistic in religion, culture, and race. Since the newer arrivals—Catholic, Jewish, and foreign-language Protestant—were largely self-contained, they did not at first affect the major assumptions of the American society, with its Anglo-Saxon common law, its English language and Protestant common schools, its Unitarian and Episcopalian and Presbyterian presidents, and the like. Since World War II, however, we have entered into a third period of American church history. Several former foreign-language Protestant churches have flowered into prominence. And the Catholic community has emerged from its minority-consciousness to a status of parity in the new multi-faith complex. So have the Jews. The election of a member of the Catholic community, now the largest church in the country, as President in 1960 was in its own way as symbolic of the breakthrough as the U.S. Supreme Court decisions in May, 1954 (school desegregation), and June, 1962 (legislative re-apportionment). The old America of white, rural, and Protestant dominance is dying. But in its death throes it has spawned some of the most wicked political movements and vicious personality types which this bloody century has seen anywhere.

The choice before the Protestant churches is clear: either they can accept the logic of a voluntaryistic and pluralistic situation, wherein lies their true genius and the appropriate area for their missionary and universalist drive, or they can end up as embittered and negative minorities which the course of history has passed by. Racialism has the same meaning where found among American Protestant churches as have the bitter anti-Catholicism and anti-Semitism which so frequently accompany it. They mark and mar a religion which has lost faith in the Author of history, which is anxiously striving to retain old ways rather than re-tool to meet the challenges of the new age.

American Nativism was first violently anti-Catholic. Fifty years later it became anti-Semitic as well. With the rise of the grandchildren of the freed Negroes to political and economic significance, and now laying claim to the free American's right to fair play in education, housing, and job opportunities, Nativism has allied with the white supremacists.

This is one of the chief practical arguments for the Protestant-Catholic dialogue, a dialogue without which this conference could not have been held. The Catholic communion is plainly a universal church, and fellowship with Catholics—which has gained such a great impetus under the leadership of Pope John XXIII—can help Protestants to avoid sinking back into racial and tribal religion. As a Catholic leader in Jamaica has put the basic premise,

> . . . the cross of Christ has created a new nation of men . . . This new nation, this sturdy race is unique in the history of mankind. It is a race created not by blood, but by grace.[17]

In the words of Pius XI's great encyclical against Nazi racialism (*Mit brennender Sorge*, 14 March 1937):

> Only superficial minds can lapse into the heresy of speaking of a national God, or a national religion; only such can make the mad attempt of trying to confine within the boundaries of a single people, within the narrow blood stream of a single race, God, the Creator of the world.[18]

More particularly, the type of Protestantism which has its chief strength in those areas most threatened by violence needs the attention to law and objective justice which is one of the strengths of Catholicism. The large churches of the Deep South stand in the tradition of sectarian Protestantism, which had, to be sure, a powerful sense of fellowship within the congregation; as for the affairs of the world, the Old Testament once sufficed these churches as a guide to righteousness and justice. This earlier appreciation of the majesty of the law rings, for example, through the messages of Abraham Lincoln. Consider these Biblically-formed words of the "Second Inaugural Address":

> Fondly do we hope, fervently do we pray, that this mighty scourge of war may speedily pass away. Yet, if God wills that it continue until all the wealth piled by the bond-man's two hundred and fifty years of unrequited toil shall be sunk, and until every drop of blood drawn with the lash shall be paid by another drawn with the sword, as was said three thousand years ago,—so still it must be said, that the judgments of the Lord are true and righteous altogether.[19]

However, with the later popularization of church membership, the abandonment of prophetic preaching, the surrender of standards of church discipline, the softening of theology and confession of faith, the Old Testament, too, was scuttled. The style of the community of grace was generalized, until at last we have a society without law and with no understanding that right is right though the heavens fall. The governor of a southern state asks the infantile question: How can a law be enforced if we don't like it? As though justice and righteousness in the social order, as though law, were conditional upon the subjective sentiments of the ill-disciplined and disobedient!

The Old Testament was the radical Protestant alternative to the tradition of natural law in Catholicism and the more conservative Protestant traditions. Without either, a society descends into anarchy. The strengthening of the Protestant-Catholic dialogue should bring to the fore the fact that the foundation of law is abiding, although men and nations may rise and fall. For my part, I am thankful that at this critical juncture we have a President of the United States who was raised to believe that law is law.

Christians and Jews

Anti-Semitism is perhaps the surest seismographic measurement of totalitarian systems and pre-totalitarian movements. The reasons are two-fold. In the first place, on the edge of the jungle the law is an especially wonderful thing! And those who represent an ancient tradition of law and order in societies where violence and anarchy are incipient are the special target of wicked men who live by chaos. More important, however, the Jews are the special objects of animosity when peoples are determined to revert to tribal religion,

> Totalitarianism appeals to the desire to return to the womb. The contrast between religion and culture imposes a strain: We escape from this strain by attempting to revert to an identity of religion and culture which prevailed at a more primitive stage; as when we indulge in alcohol as an anodyne, we consciously seek unconsciousness.[20]

Whether personally religious or not, the Jew by his very existence represents the God of Abraham, Isaac, and Jacob and His authorship of world history. This is what the baptized also stand for in their baptismal and confirmation vows. But when totalitarian movements arise, the Gentile can take on protective coloration: he can apostatize, revert to a more primitive stage, betray his baptism. The Jew cannot. It can be truly said that those millions of Jews who suffered and died in Hitler's Europe were martyred for what the Christians would have been martyred for had they stayed Christian. In a mysterious way, both in disaster and in creativity, the Jews and the Christians are united in a common destiny.

It is not accident, but a dreadful portent, that precisely at the moment when White Citizens' Councils, Circuit Riders, Minutemen, John Birchers, and all the denizens of the political underworld are uniting to attack the Supreme Court, the President, and the remaining centers of free discussion among the churches, the universities, and the trade unions, synagogues should be bombed in our cities.

Christians are "spiritual Semites." They know that tribal religion apart from the Biblical tradition is dangerous, because they understand their own true history. For that matter, many of us in the "Christian Israel" believe that God's providence for his "first Israel" is by no means exhausted. Reversions to pre-baptismal tribalism, whether "the southern way of life" or *des deutsche Volkswesen* of the Nazis, are rooted in hatred of the Church and her claims, even though the Jews are often the first victims of the revolt out of the abyss.

Negroes and Whites

Catholics, and even an occasional Jew, can sometimes be conned into embracing the reactionary legend of America's past. After all, Mr. Welch assures us half of the members of his conspiracy are Catholics! But there is one minority which cannot blind its eyes by backward-looking legends, a minority which knows that every leap in social progress and in self-realization must be suffered through as the distance runner fights through to his "second wind." "The American Negro," as Mr. James Baldwin has pointed out, "has the great advantage of having never believed that collection of myths to which white Americans cling: that their ancestors were all freedom-loving heroes, that they were born in the greatest country the world has ever seen. . . ."[21] Our Negro citizens know, in short, that we are creatures, and not gods; and in a world where most of the wickedness toward persons had been inspired by pride (*superbia, hubris*) and committed under the "Jehovah complex," this is a precious wisdom. When America struggles through to a mature self-realization, subduing regressive tendencies both religious and political, it will be in good part thanks to the American Negro.

At the present time the Negro citizen is the butt of most of the anxieties of our society, a society which has often demonstrated its buoyancy in the crusade but has not yet developed the steadiness for the long haul. When Germany regressed into heathenism in the Third Reich, anti-Semitism became the

> face of aggressive and chauvinistic nationalism turned inward toward the nation itself. . . . During the period of successful imperialism the face was turned outward, toward the British, French, Slavs, Chinese, Africans. When the march towards a place in the sun was stopped, anti-Semitism, the "twin brother" of extreme German nationalism, made the defeated nation itself the new battle-ground and re-defined the enemy.[22]

In America, the wickedness of the frustrated and insecure is directed primarily against the Negro. As an acute Negro observer has recently written:

> I do not know many Negroes who are eager to be "accepted" by white people, still less to be loved by them; they, the blacks, simply don't wish to be beaten over the head by the whites every instant of our brief passage on this planet. White people in this country will have quite enough to do in learning how to accept and love themselves and each other, and when they have achieved this—which will not be tomorrow and may very well be never—the Negro problem will no longer exist, for it will no longer be needed.[23]

If the miracle of *agape*, of brotherhood-love, were not to come, if Americans prove incapable of breaking out of their several ghettos, then the judgment has already been passed upon us. Then the "faceless" ones—the cowardly fashioners

of the terrorists' plastic bombs, the organizers of anonymous
campaigns, the conspirators who attack our fundamental institutions, the nightriders with their shotgun assaults on citizens,
the vile maggots which feed everywhere so that social and
political putrefaction go unhealed—will inherit the wasteland
and the jungle.

> I call heaven and earth to record this day against you, that
> I have set before you life and death, blessing and cursing:
> therefore choose life, that both thou and thy seed may live.
> (Deut. 30:19)

The Great City

The third age of religion in America is the Great City,
beginning with a pluralism in religion, race, and culture.

Seventy–five years ago, four out of five Americans lived on
farms or in rural villages. Today, over 25% live in the twelve
largest metropolitan areas and over 50% are concentrated in
220 counties (out of over 3000). Eighty percent of the population resides within twenty-five miles of cities of at least 25,000.
"Religion today is challenged to create an urban civilization."[24]
Technologically, we can no longer live without each other.
Our liberty, too, has become indivisible. The word on our wall
is this: "Communicate, or perish!"

Communication between real persons, persons with names
and faces, persons freed from false images of themselves and
of the others, is the necessary foundation for creative love—for
the miracle to occur which transcends and transmutes all our
natural impossibilities into the City Beautiful. By the same
token, totalitarian movements can be identified by their hostility to full, free, and informed discussion. Beware the hooded
riders, the anonymous tale-bearers; those without names
and without faces! The faceless ones are the enemies of all

free men. The problem is national, indeed international. But every local battle which is fought through to bring persons face to face who share a common destiny, which breaks some anxious group out of the sound-proofed room of fear and hate, is a victory for everyone everywhere—whatever his credal, cultural, or racial background—who looks hopefully to the day when every American may say with meaning: "I was born free!" (Acts 22:28)

NOTES

1. *Dallas Morning News* (12/16/62), Sec. 3, p. 1.
2. Rev. Duncan M. Gray, Jr. (Protestant Episcopal), Rev. Murphy C. Wilds (Southern Presbyterian), and Rev. Wayne Coleman (Southern Baptist); *New York Times* (10/8/62), p. 15.
3. Cf. the author's *From State Church to Pluralism* (New York: Doubleday & Co., 1962), Introduction.
4. Ferlinghetti, Lawrence, "I am Waiting" from *Coney Island of the Mind* (New York: New Directions).
5. Smith, Timothy L., *Revivalism and Social Reform* (New York & Nashville: Abingdon Press, 1957), p. 12.
6. Smith, Elwyn A., "The Role of the South in the Presbyterian Schism of 1837-38," XXIX *Church History* (1960) 1:44-63, quotation on p. 57.
7. Thornwell, J. H., *The Rights and Duties of Masters* (Charleston, S.C.: Walker & James, 1850), p. 8.
8. *Ibid.*, p. 14.
9. Cf. the author's *The Free Church* (Boston: Beacon Press, 1957), p. 117.
10. Haselden, Kyle, *The Racial Problem in Christian Perspective* (New York: Harper & Bros., 1959); Maston, T. B., *Segregation and Desegregation: A Christian Approach* (New York: Macmillan Co., 1959).
11. Marais, Ben J., "The Race Question: The U.S. and South Africa," XXII *Christianity and Crisis* (1962) 18:187-89.
12. Stoddard, Lathrop, *The Rising Tide of Color* (New York: Charles Scribner's Sons, 1920). A representative "scientific"

statement: "In the western hemisphere there are some 25,000,000 persons of more or less mixed black blood, brought thither in modern times as slaves by the white conquerors of the New World. Still, whatever may be the destiny of these transplanted black folk, the black man's chief significance, from the world aspect, must remain bound up with the great nucleus of negro population in the African homeland." pp. 87-88

13. Grant, Madison, *The Passing of the Great Race* (New York: Charles Scribner's Sons, 1924), 4th revised edition. A leader in the New York Zoological Society, American Museum of Natural History, American Geographical Society, etc., Grant's fear of the "mongrelization" of the blue-eyed, blond-haired "Nordic race" led him to such representative statements as these: "The church assumes a serious responsibility toward the future of the race whenever it steps in and preserves a defective strain . . ." (p. 49). "In mankind it would not be a matter of great difficuty to secure a general consensus of public opinion as to the least desirable, let us say, ten per cent of the community. When this unemployed and unemployable human residuum has been eliminated. . . ." (p. 54). The Preface to Grant's book was written by a distinguished professor at Columbia University. Since Adolf Hitler, such views are encountered chiefly in the underbrush of the academic world; cf. John O. Beaty's *The Iron Curtain Over America* (Dallas: Wilkinson Publ. Co., 1951), or Stuart Omer Landry's *The Cult of Equality* (New Orleans: Pelikan Publ. Co., 1945). Nevertheless, such volumes as these—with their poor printing, careless footnotes, and wildly undisciplined speculation—still pass for learning in some circles. "In the kingdom of the blind, the one-eyed man is king."

14. Campbell, Ernest G., and Pettigrew, Thomas F., *Christians in Racial Crisis: A Sstudy of Little Rock's Ministry* (Washington: Public Affairs Press, 1959), pp. 137–70.

15. Haselden, Kyle, *op. cit.*, p. 33.

16. Hayes Beall in LXII *The Christian Century* (1945) 29:840.

17. LaFarge, John, *The Catholic Viewpoint on Race Relations* (Garden City, N.Y.: Hanover House, 1956), quotation on p. 111.

18. *Ibid.*, pp. 82–83.

19. In Sandburg, Carl, *Abraham Lincoln, III: The War Years, 1864–65* (New York: Dell Publ. Co., 1959), pp. 771–73.

20. Quoted from T. S. Eliot's *Notes Towards the Definition of*

Culture (p. 68), in Braybrooke, Neville, ed., *T. S. Eliot: A Symposium for His Seventieth Birthday* (New York: Farrar, Straus & Co., 1958).

21. Baldwin, James, "Letter from a Region in My Mind," *The New Yorker* (11/17/62), pp. 59ff, 142.
22. Massing, Paul, *Rehearsal for Destruction* (New York: Harper & Bros., 1949), p. 147, quoting Franz Oppenheimer.
23. Baldwin, James, *loc. cit.*, p. 60.
24. Osman, John, "A City is a Civilization," in Lee, Robert, ed., *Cities and the Churches* (Philadelphia: Westminister Press, 1962), p. 75.

PART III

....

*The Religious Basis of
Equality of Opportunity—
The Segregation of God*

The Religious Basis of
Equality of Opportunity—
The Segregation of God

RABBI ABRAHAM J. HESCHEL

I

At the first conference on religion and race, the main participants were Pharaoh and Moses. Moses' words were: "Thus says the Lord, the God of Israel, let My people go that they may celebrate a feast to Me." While Pharaoh retorted: "Who is the Lord, that I should heed this voice and let Israel go? I do not know the Lord, and moreover I will not let Israel go."

The outcome of that summit meeting has not come to an end. Pharaoh is not ready to capitulate. The exodus began, but is far from having been completed. In fact, it was easier for the children of Israel to cross the Red Sea than for a Negro to cross certain university campuses.

Let us dodge no issues. Let us yield no inch to bigotry, let us make no compromise with callousness.

In the words of William Lloyd Garrison, "I will be as harsh as truth, and as uncompromising as justice. On this subject [slavery] I do not wish to think, to speak, or to write with moderation. I am in earnest—I will not equivocate—I will not excuse—I will not retreat a single inch—and I will be heard."

Religion and race. How can the two be uttered together? To act in the spirit of religion is to unite what lies apart, to remember that humanity as a whole is God's beloved child.

To act in the spirit of race is to sunder, to slash, to dismember the flesh of living humanity. Is this the way to honor a father: to torture his child? How can we hear the word race and feel no self-reproach?

Race as a *normative* legal or political concept is capable of expanding to formidable dimensions. A mere thought, it extends to become a way of thinking, a highway of insolence, as well as a standard of values, overriding truth, justice, beauty. As a standard of values and behavior, race operates as a comprehensive doctrine, as racism. And racism is worse than idolatry. *Racism is satanism,* unmitigated evil.

Few of us seem to realize how insidious, how radical, how universal an evil racism is. Few of us realize that racism is man's gravest threat to man, the maximum of hatred for a minimum of reason, the maximum of cruelty for a minimum of thinking.

Perhaps this Conference should have been called *Religion or Race.* You cannot worship God and at the same time look at man as if he were a horse.

Shortly before he died, Moses spoke to his people. "I call heaven and earth to witness against you this day: I have set before you life and death, blessing and curse. *Choose life.*" (Deuteronomy 30:19). The aim of this conference is first of all to state clearly the stark alternative. I call heaven and earth to witness against you this day: I have set before you religion and race, life and death, blessing and curse. Choose life.

"Race prejudice, a universal human ailment, is the most recalcitrant aspect of the evil in man" (Reinhold Niebuhr), a treacherous denial of the existence of God.

What is an idol? *Any god who is mine but not yours,* any god concerned with me but not with you, *is an idol.*

Faith in God is not simply *an afterlife-insurance policy. Racial or religious bigotry* must be recognized for what it is: *blasphemy.*

In several ways man is set apart from all beings created in six days. The Bible does not say, God created the plant or the animal; it says, God created *different* kinds of plants, *different kinds* of animals (Genesis 1: 11–12, 21–25). In striking contrast, it does not say, God created different kinds of man, men of different colors and races; it proclaims, God created one single man. From one single man all men are descended.

To think of man in terms of white, black or yellow is more than an error. It is *an eye disease, a cancer of the soul.*

The redeeming quality of man lies in his ability to sense his kinship with all men. Yet there is a deadly poison that inflames the eye, making us see the generality of race but not the uniqueness of the human face. Pigmentation is what counts. The Negro is a stranger to many souls. There are people in our country whose moral sensitivity suffers a black-out when confronted with the black man's predicament.

How many disasters do we have to go through in order to realize that all of humanity has a stake in the liberty of one person; whenever one person is offended, we are all hurt. What begins as inequality of some inevitably ends as inequality of all.

In referring to the Negro in this paper we must, of course, always keep equally in mind the plight of all individuals belonging to a racial, religious, ethnic or cultural minority.

This Conference should dedicate itself not only to the problem of the Negro but also to the problem of the white man, not only to the plight of the colored but also to the situation of the white people, to the cure of a disease affecting the spiritual substance and condition of every one of us. What we need is an NAAAP, a National Association for the Advancement of All People. Prayer and prejudice cannot dwell in the same heart. Worship without compassion is worse than self-deception; it is an abomination.

Thus the problem is not only how to do justice to the colored people, it is also how to stop the profanation of God's name by dishonoring the Negro's name.

One hundred years ago the emancipation was proclaimed. It is time for the white man to strive for *self-emancipation*, to set himself free of bigotry, to stop being a slave to wholesale contempt, a passive recipient of slander.

II

"I saw all the oppressions that are practiced under the sun. Behold, the tears of the oppressed, they had no one to comfort them! On the side of the oppressors there was power, and there was no one to comfort them." (Ecclesiastes 4:1)

There is a form of oppression which is more painful and more scathing than physical injury or economic privation. It is *public humiliation*. What afflicts my conscience is that my face, whose skin happens not to be dark, instead of radiating the likeness of God, has come to be taken as an image of haughty assumption and overbearance. Whether justified or not, I, the white man, have become in the eyes of others a symbol of arrogance and pretension, giving offense to other human beings, hurting their pride, even without intending it. My very presence inflicting insult!

My heart is sick when I think of the anguish and the sighs, of the quiet tears shed in the nights in the overcrowded dwellings in the slums of our great cities, of the pangs of despair, of the cup of humiliation that is running over.

The crime of murder is tangible and punishable by law. The sin of insult is imponderable, invisible. When blood is shed, human eyes see red; when a heart is crushed, it is only God who shares the pain.

In the Hebrew language one word denotes both crimes. Bloodshed is the word that denotes both murder and humiliation. The law demands: one should rather be killed than commit murder. Piety demands: one should rather commit suicide than offend a person publicly. It is better, the Talmud insists, to throw oneself alive into a burning furnace than to humiliate a human being publicly.

He who commits a major sin may repent and be forgiven. But he who offends a person publicly will have no share in the life to come.

It is not within the power of God to forgive the sins committed toward men. We must first ask for forgiveness of those whom our society has wronged before asking for the forgiveness of God.

Daily we patronize institutions which are visible manifestations of arrogance toward those whose skin differs from mine. Daily we cooperate with people who are guilty of active discrimination.

How long will I continue to be tolerant of, even participant in, acts of embarrassing and humiliating human beings, in restaurants, hotels, buses, or parks, employment agencies, public schools and universities? One ought rather be shamed than put others to shame.

Our Rabbis taught: "Those who are insulted but do not insult, hear themselves reviled without answering, act through love and rejoice in suffering, of them Scripture says: 'They who love the Lord are as the sun when rising in full splendor.'" (Judges 5:31)

Let us cease to be apologetic, cautious, timid. Racial tension and strife is both sin and punishment. *The Negro's plight*, the blighted areas in the large cities, are they not the fruit of our sins?

By negligence and silence we have all become accessory before the God of mercy to the injustice committed against the Negroes by men of our nation. Our derelictions are many.

We have failed to demand, to insist, to challenge, to chastise.

In the words of Thomas Jefferson, "I tremble for my country when I reflect that God is just."

III

There are several ways of dealing with our bad conscience. 1) We can extenuate our responsibility; 2) we can keep the Negro out of our sight; 3) we can alleviate our qualms by pointing to the progress made; 4) we can delegate the responsibility to the courts; 5) we can silence our conscience by cultivating indifference; 6) we can dedicate our minds to issues of a far more sublime nature.

1) Modern thought has a tendency to extenuate personal responsibility. Understanding the complexity of human nature, the inter-relationship of individual and society, of consciousness and the subconscious, we find it difficult to isolate the deed from the circumstances in which it was done. Our enthusiasm is easily stunned by realizing the ramifications and complexity of the problem we face and the enormous obstacles we encounter in trying to implement the philosophy affirmed in the 13th and 14th Amendments as well as in the 1954 decision of the Supreme Court. Yet this general tendency, for all its important correctives and insights, has often had the effect of obscuring our essential vision, aiding our conscience to grow scales: excuses, pretense, self-pity. The sense of guilt may disappear; no crime is absolute, no sin devoid of apology. Within the limits of the human mind, relativity may be true and merciful. Yet the mind's scope embraces but a fragment of society, a few instants of history; it thinks of what has happened, it is unable to imagine what might have happened. The qualms of my conscience are easrily cured—even while the agony for which I am accountable continues unabated.

2) Another way of dealing with a bad conscience is to keep the Negro out of sight.

The Word proclaims: Love thy neighbor! *So we make it impossible for him to be a neighbor.* Let a Negro move into our neighborhood and madness overtakes the residents. To quote a recent editorial in the *Christian Century* (12–26–62):

> The ghettoization of the Negro in American society is increasing. Three million Negroes—roughly one-sixth of the nation's Negro population—are now congested in five of the greatest metropolitan centers of the north. The alienation of the Negro from the mainstream of American life proceeds space. The Negro is discovering to his sorrow that the mobility which he gained in the Emancipation Proclamation and the 13th and 14th Amendments to the Constitution nearly a hundred years ago merely enables him to move from one ghetto to another. A partial apartheid—economic, social, political and religious—continues to be enforced by the white people of the U.S. They use various pressures—some open, some covert—to keep the Negro isolated from the nation's social, cultural and religious community, the result being black islands surrounded by a vast white sea. Such enclaves in American society not only destroy the cohesiveness of the nation but also offend the Negro's dignity and restrict his opportunity. These segregated islands are also an embarrassment to white people who want an open society but are trapped by a system they despise. Restricted housing is the chief offender. So long as the racially exclusive patterns of suburban America continue, the Negro will remain an exile in his own land.

3) To some Americans the situation of the Negro, for all its stains and spots, seems fair and trim. So many revolutionary changes have taken place in the field of civil rights, so many deeds of charity are being done; so much decency radiates day and night. Our standards are modest; our sense of injustice tolerable, timid; our moral indignation impermanent; yet

human violence is interminable, unbearable, permanent. The conscience builds its confines, is subject to fatigue, it longs for comfort. Yet those who are hurt, and He Who inhabits eternity, neither slumber nor sleep.

4) Most of us are content to delegate the problem to the courts, as if justice were a matter for professionals or specialists. But to do justice is what God demands of every man: it is the supreme commandment, and one that cannot be fulfilled vicariously.

Righteousness must dwell not only in the places where justice is judicially administered. There are many ways of evading the law and escaping the arm of justice. Only a few acts of violence are brought to the attention of the courts. As a rule, those who know how to exploit are endowed with the skill to justify their acts, while those who are easily exploited possess no skill in pleading their own cause. Those who neither exploit nor are exploited are ready to fight when their own interests are harmed; they will not be involved when not personally affected. Who shall plead for the helpless? Who shall prevent the epidemic of injustice that no court of justice is capable of stopping?

In a sense, the calling of the prophet may be described as that of an advocate or champion, speaking for those who are too weak to plead their own cause. Indeed, the major activity of the prophets was *interference*, remonstrating about wrongs inflicted on other people, meddling in affairs which were seemingly neither their concern nor their responsibility. A prudent man is he who minds his own business, staying away from questions which do not involve his own interests, particularly when not authorized to step in—and prophets were given no mandate by the widows and orphans to plead their cause. The prophet is a person who is not tolerant of wrongs done to others, who resents other people's injuries. He even calls upon others to be the champions of the poor. It is to every member of the community, not alone to the judges, that Isaiah directs his plea:

> Seek justice,
> Undo oppression;
> Defend the fatherless,
> Plead for the widow.
> Isaiah 1:17

5) There is an evil which most of us condone and are even guilty of: *indifference to evil*. We remain neutral, impartial, and not easily moved by the wrongs done unto other people. Indifference to evil is more insidious than evil itself; it is more universal, more contagious, more dangerous. A silent justification, it makes possible an evil erupting as an exception becoming the rule and being in turn accepted.

The prophets' great contribution to humanity was the discovery of *the evil of indifference*. One may be decent and sinister, pious and sinful.

The prophet is a person who suffers the harms done to others. Wherever a crime is committed, it is as if the prophet were the victim and the prey. The prophet's angry words cry. The wrath of God is a lamentation. All prophecy is one great exclamation; God is not indifferent to evil! He is always concerned, He is personally affected by what man does to man. He is a God of pathos.

6) In condemning the clergymen who joined Dr. Martin Luther King in protesting against local statutes and practices which denied constitutional liberties to groups of citizens on account of race, a white preacher declared: "The job of the minister is to lead the souls of men to God, not to bring about confusion by getting tangled up in transitory social problems."

In contrast to this definition, the prophets passionately proclaim that God Himself is concerned with "the transitory social problems," with the blights of society, with the affairs of the market place.

What is the essence of being a prophet? *A prophet is a person who holds God and men in one thought at one time, at all times.* Our tragedy begins with *the segregation of God,* with the bifurcation of the secular and sacred. We worry more about the purity of dogma than about the *integrity of love.* *We think of God in the past tense* and refuse to realize that *God is always present* and *never, never past*; that God may be more intimately *present in slums than in mansions, with those who are smarting under the abuse of the callous.*

There are, of course, many among us whose record in dealing with the Negroes and other minority groups is unspotted. However, an honest estimation of the moral state of our society will disclose: *Some are guilty, but all are responsible.* If we admit that the individual is in some measure conditioned or affected by the public climate of opinion, an individual's crime discloses society's corruption. In a community not indifferent to suffering, uncompromisingly impatient with cruelty and falsehood, racial discrimination would be infrequent rather than common.

IV

That equality is a good thing, a fine goal, may be generally accepted. What is lacking is a sense of the *monstrosity of inequality.* Seen from the perspective of prophetic faith, the predicament of justice is the predicament of God.

Of course, more and more people are becoming aware of the Negro problem, but they fail to grasp its being a personal problem. People are increasingly fearful of social tension and disturbance. However, so long as our society is more concerned to prevent racial strife than to prevent humiliation, the cause of strife, its moral status will be depressing, indeed.

The history of inter-racial relations is a nightmare. Equality of all men, a platitude to some minds, remains a scandal to many hearts. Inequality is the ideal setting for the abuse of power, a perfect justification for man's cruelty to man. Equality is an obstacle to callousness, setting a limit to power. Indeed, the history of mankind may be described as the history of the tension between power and equality.

Equality is an inter-personal relationship, involving both a claim and a recognition. My claim to equality has its logical basis in the recognition of my fellow men's identical claim. Do I not forfeit my own rights by denying to my fellow men the rights I claim for myself?

It is not humanity that endows the sky with inalienable stars. It is not society that bestows upon every man his inalienable rights. Equality of all men is not due to man's innocence or virtue. Equality of man is due to *God's love and commitment to all men*.

The ultimate worth of man is due neither to his virtue nor to his faith. *It is due to God's virtue, to God's faith. Wherever you see a trace of man, there is the presence of God.* From the perspective of eternity our recognition of equality of all men seems as generous an act as the acknowledgment that stars and planets have a right to be.

How can I withhold from others what does not belong to me?

Equality as a religious commandment goes beyond the principle of equality before the law. Equality as a religious commandment means *personal involvement*, fellowship, mutual reverence and concern. It means my being hurt when a Negro is offended. It means that I am bereaved whenever a Negro is *disfranchised*.

The shotgun blasts that have been fired at the house of

James Meredith's father in Kosciusko, Mississippi, make us cry for shame wherever we are.

There is no insight more disclosing: *God is One, and humanity is one.* There is no possibility more frightening: God's name may be desecrated.

God is every man's pedigree. He is either the Father of all men or of no man. The image of God is either in every man or in no man.

From the point of view of moral philosophy it is our duty to have regard for every man. Yet such regard is contingent upon the moral merit of the particular man. From the point of view of religious philosophy it is our duty to have regard and compassion for every man regardless of his moral merit. God's covenant is with all men, and we must never be oblivious of *the equality of the divine dignity* of all men. The image of God is in the criminal as well as in the saint. How could my regard for man be contingent upon his merit, if I know that in the eyes of God I myself may be without merit!

You shall not make yourself a graven image or any likeness of God. The making and worshipping of images is considered an abomination, vehemently condemned in the Bible. The world and God are not of the same essence. There can be no man-made symbols of God.

And yet there is something in the world that the Bible does regard as a symbol of God. It is not a temple nor a tree, it is not a statue nor a star. *The symbol of God is man,* every man. How significant is the fact that the term *tselem* which is frequently used in a damnatory sense for a man-made image of God, as well as the term *demuth*, likeness—of which Isaiah claims (48:18), no *demuth* can be applied to God—are employed in denoting man as an image and likeness of God. Man, every man, must be treated with the honor due to a likeness representing the King of kings.

He who oppresses a poor man insults his Maker,
He who is kind to the needy honors Him.

Proverbs 14:31; cf. 17:15

V

The way we act, the way we fail to act is a disgrace which must not go on forever. This is not a white man's world. This is not a colored man's world. It is God's world. No man has a place in this world who tries to keep another man in his place. It is time for the white man to repent. We have failed to use the avenues open to us to educate the hearts and minds of men, to identify ourselves with those who are underprivileged. But repentance is more than contrition and remorse for sins, for harms done. Repentance means a new insight, a new spirit. It also means a course of action.

Racism is an evil of tremendous power, but God's will transcends all powers. Surrender to despair is surrender to evil. It is important to feel anxiety, it is sinful to wallow in despair.

What we need is a total mobilization of heart, intelligence, and wealth for the purpose of love and justice. God is in search of men, waiting, hoping for man to do His will.

The most practical thing is not to weep but to act and to have faith in God's assistance and grace in our trying to do His will.

This world, this society can be redeemed. God has a stake in our moral predicament. I cannot believe that God will be defeated.

What we face is a human emergency. It will require much devotion, wisdom, and divine grace to eliminate that massive sense of inferiority, the creeping bitterness. It will require a high quality of imaginative sympathy, sustained cooperation both in thought and in action, by individuals as well as by institutions, to weed out memories of frustration, roots of resentment.

We must act even when inclination and vested interests should militate against equality. Human self-interest is often our Nemesis! It is the audacity of faith that redeems us. To have faith is to be ahead of one's normal thoughts, to transcend confused motivations, to lift oneself by one's bootstraps. Mere knowledge or belief is too feeble to be a cure of man's hostility to man, of man's tendency to fratricide. The only remedy is *personal sacrifice*: to abandon, to reject what seems dear and even plausible for the sake of the greater truth; to do more than I am ready to understand for the sake of God. Required is a breakthrough, a *leap of action*. It is the deed that will purify the heart. It is the deed that will sanctify the mind. The deed is the test, the trial, and the risk.

The plight of the Negro must become our most important concern. Seen in the light of our religious tradition, *the Negro problem is God's gift to America*, the test of our integrity, a magnificent spiritual opportunity.

Humanity can only thrive when challenged, when called upon to answer new demands, to reach out for new heights. Imagine how smug, complacent, vapid, and foolish we would be, if we had to subsist on prosperity alone. It is for us to understand that religion is not sentimentality, that God is not a patron. Religion is a demand, God is a challenge, speaking to us in the language of human situations. His voice is in the dimension of history.

The universe is done. The greater masterpiece still undone, still in the process of being created, is history. For accomplishing His grand design, God needs the help of man. Man is and has the instrument of God, which he may or may not use in consonance with the grand design. Life is clay, and righteousness the mold in which God wants history to be shaped. But human beings, instead of fashioning the clay, deform the shape. God needs mercy, righteousness; His needs cannot be satisfied in space, by sitting in pews, by visiting temples, but in history, in time. It is within the realm of history that man is charged with God's mission.

There are those who maintain that the situation is too grave for us to do much about it, that whatever we might do would be "too little and too late," that the most practiced thing we can do is "to weep" and to despair. If such a message is true, then God has spoken in vain.

Such a message is 4000 years too late. It is good Babylonian theology. In the meantime, certain things have happened: Abraham, Moses, the Prophets, the Christian Gospel.

History is not all darkness. It was good that Moses did not study theology under the teachers of that message; otherwise, I would still be in Egypt building pyramids. Abraham was all alone in a world of paganism; the difficulties he faced were hardly less grave than ours.

The greatest heresy is despair, despair of men's power for goodness, men's power for love.

It is not enough for us to exhort the Government. What we must do is to set an example, not merely to acknowledge the Negro but to welcome him, not grudgingly but joyously, to take delight in enabling him to enjoy what is due to him. We are all *Pharaohs* or *slaves of Pharaohs*. It is sad to be a slave of Pharaoh. *It is horrible to be a Pharaoh.*

Daily we should take account and ask: What have I done today *to alleviate the anguish, to mitigate the evil, to prevent humiliation?*

Let there be a grain of prophet in every man!

Our concern must be expressed not symbolically, but literally; not only publicly, but also *privately*; not only occasionally, but regularly.

What we need is the involvement of everyone of us as individuals. What we need is *restlessness*, a constant awareness of the monstrosity of injustice.

The concern for the dignity of the Negro must be an explicit tenet of our creeds. He who offends a Negro, whether as a landowner or employer, whether as waiter or sales-girl, is guilty of offending the majesty of God. No minister or layman has a right to question the principle that reverence for God is shown in reverence for man, that the fear we must feel lest we hurt or humiliate a human being must be as unconditional as fear of God. An act of violence is an act of desecration. To be arrogant toward man is to be blasphemous toward God.

In the words of Pope John XXIII, when opening the Twenty-first Ecumenical Council, "divine Providence is leading us to a new order of human relations." History has made us all neighbors. The age of moral mediocrity and complacency has run out. This is a time for radical commitment, for radical action.

Let us not forget the story of the sons of Jacob. Joseph, the dreamer of dreams, was sold into slavery by his own brothers. But at the end it was Joseph who rose to be the saviour of those who had sold him into captivity.

Mankind lies groaning, afflicted by fear, frustration and despair. Perhaps it is the will of God that among the Josephs of the future there will be many who have once been slaves and whose skin is dark. The great spiritual resources of the Negroes, their capacity for joy, their quiet nobility, their attachment to the Bible, their power of worship and enthusiasm, may prove a blessing to all mankind.

In the words of the prophet Amos (5:24):

> Let justice roll down like waters,
> And righteousness like a mighty stream.

A mighty stream, expressive of the vehemence of a never-ending, surging, fighting movement—as if obstacles had to be washed away for justice to be done. No rock is so hard that water cannot pierce it. "The mountain falls and crumbles away, the rock is removed from its place—the waters wear away the stones." (Job 14:18 f.) Justice is not a mere norm, but a fighting challenge, a restless drive.

Righteousness as a mere tributary, feeding the immense stream of human interests, is easily exhausted and more easily abused. But righteousness is not a trickle; it is God's power in the world, a torrent, an impetous drive, full of grandeur and majesty. The surge is choked, the sweep is blocked. Yet the mighty stream will break all dikes.

Justice, people seem to agree, is a principle, a norm, an ideal of the highest importance. We all insist that it ought to be—but it may not be. In the eyes of the prophets, justice is more than an idea or a norm: justice is charged with the omnipotence of God. What ought to be, shall be!

PART IV

....

*The Religious Institution
and the Community*

The Role of Church and Synagogue in the Racially Changing Community

DR. DAN W. DODSON

I. *The Nature of the Change*

The most continuously significant confrontation to face organized religion on the domestic scene during the past two
decades is undoubtedly that of the racially changing community. The last World War, the mechanization of agricul-
ture, the use of rubber for transportation and the septic tank
have produced a revolution in neighborhood design. Marginal
populations have been drawn away from the farms and located in the heart of major cities. The suburbs have expanded
enormously to accommodate the middle class, largely white
population, which has withdrawn from cities.

The need for cheap, unskilled labor, plus Castro's revolution, has accounted for the emigration of large numbers of
Spanish-speaking peoples from both the Caribbean coasts and
from Mexico. Like the Negro population of rural America
which has been the principal source of domestic migration to
the cities, these newcomers have tended to settle in urban
areas, with the exception of those who are seasonally employed
as migrant laborers on farms.

The extent of the revolution brought about by these changes
can be estimated when it is understood that between 1950 and

1960 the racial composition of the following states changed as follows:

TABLE I

Change in Negro Population of Select States 1950-1960

	1950	1960	Change
New York	918,191	1,417,511	499,320
California	462,172	883,861	421,689
Michigan	442,296	717,581	275,285
Illinois	645,980	1,037,470	391,490
New Jersey	318,565	514,875	196,310
Ohio	513,072	786,097	273,025

New York State now has the largest Negro population of any of the fifty states, and Illinois is among the top five in rank of Negro inhabitants, exceeded only by New York, Texas, Georgia, North Carolina and Louisiana. The cities with the largest Negro concentrations by rank are: New York City (1,087,931), Chicago (812,637), Philadelphia (529,240), Detroit (482,223), Washington, D.C. (411,737), Los Angeles (334,916) and Baltimore (326,589). So it is evident that marginal populations have moved away from rural into large metropolitan area, and from the South to the North, West and East.

Within the cities this indicates that the trend has been for the middle income whites to move to the suburbs leaving such vacancies to be replaced by an influx of Negroes and Spanish-speaking emigrants. For the most part the former group is prominent because of distinctive color. Consequently it is not possible for them to escape detection by learning the manners and customs of the dominant group as did the previous minorities. Neither is it possible to conceal the plight of such persons among them who suffer the trauma of slum shock and degradation occasioned by the discrimination and prejudice evidenced toward them. The worst social problems America faces are now in the heart of her cities—the show places of the country. Social problems are no longer hidden on the plantations of the Mississippi Delta.

This transformation of the city has also led to rapid, and sometimes cataclysmic changes within neighborhoods. One settlement house with which this speaker worked was located in such an area. Its leadership thought there might be as many as ten per cent Puerto Ricans within its environs. Our study indicated that actually it was already 45 per cent, so rapidly had the change come about. In the suburbs the change in racial composition has been more diffuse, but nevertheless pronounced. As Negroes acquire middle class status, they tend to migrate suburbanward also. The disturbances in Levittown, Pennsylvania, and Deerfield, Illinois, indicate the kinds of resistance which has been shown to this *avant garde*.

II. Issues in Community Change

An examination of the issues in change suggest some of the problems which confront churches in dealing with it. Among these are:

(1) All communities are constantly changing. What is referred to here is either the rate of change or the nature of the change. Sometimes it is both.

(2) A community with a well-regulated rate of change develops a power structure; norms of behavior are achieved and newcomers are assimilated into this milieu. This means that the community moves to solve its problems through integrative processes rather than through conflict. However, when a com-

munity changes quickly or the change is radical in nature, the power group arms to defend itself, with the consequence that new arrivals must necessarily move through conflict to make their voices heard in decision-making processes. This is thought to be un-Christian and disruptive in most instances.

(3) The established churches of the communities-in-change were built and are operated by the power or status groups. These frequently feel that their institutions belong to the congregation rather than to God. Hence, the local congregation has difficulty in dealing with the confrontations which accompany new viewpoints. The denomination or faith formulates inspiring statements relating to equality and spiritual fraternity. But these statements are ideals in the abstract and are difficult to apply concretely when the community is in crisis. Too often significant religious leaders are reduced to the position of the pastors who, in Little Rock, during the crisis, called a prayer meeting to pray that God's Will be done. A study of one denomination indicated that the stronger the statement prepared by the hierarchy of the denomination, the less it was subscribed to by parishoners!

(4) When neighborhoods begin to alter, it is generally those with children which are most affected. Families with children are first to leave, and families with children the first to arrive. This exchange has two significant implications. The first is that erroneous impressions about the extent of change are gathered, simply because children are out and about more than are adults. Peak demands are placed upon institutional facilities for service, thus sharpening the contrast between those who have access to services and those who do not. Secondly, the differential of change leaves in a community

those who are least adaptible to change, and who possess institutional control to keep it from happening. Instances are numerous in which a church was not able to change its membership policies until some patriarch who was extremely influential was deceased. By this time, all too often, the institution had declined too far ever to be resurrected.

(5) Other things being equal, those populations who do not patronize public schools stay longer in a changing community than those who depend upon these facilities. In a dispute in the Bedford Stuyvesant area of Brooklyn concerning sending white children to school in an all-Negro neighborhood, the district superintendent of schools reported that there were more white children attending non-public schools within walking distance of the junior high school in dispute, than there were white children in all the public schools of the district. The same pattern was discovered in New Rochelle's Washington and Columbus elementary schools. Whyte observed the same situation in the Rittenhouse Square section of Philadelphia and the Bolton Hill district of Baltimore. It is not that these religious and private schools discriminate against Negroes, but rather that new residents are either not religiously or economically attracted to them.

(6) Another characteristic of rapid community change is that incoming groups bring their indigenous institutions with them. Great difficulty in sharing existing voluntary agencies, including the church, accompanies these attitudes. Many congregations have "opened their doors" and extended welcomes only to find that the in-coming group was not attracted to their kind of fellowship. This has been a source of disappointment to many congregations. However, it should be no sur-

prise. One of the problems of such in-coming groups is their distrust of the motives of the dominant group. Too often proffered services and a welcome are really thinly veiled attempts to proselytize newcomers, using the resources of established services as "bait." Possibly, both evangelical faiths, the Protestant and the Roman Catholic, serve as valid illustrations. For example, the Roman Catholic group, which in the East has fewer Negro adherents, makes an all-out drive for the Negroes and neglects its Spanish parishoners, for whom it has a larger responsibility. The Protestants on the other hand, appear anxious to serve the Puerto Ricans and Mexicans, and neglect their major constituency, the Negroes. Be that as it may, many of both persuasions are in conflict concerning how best to fulfill their Christian mandate without having their efforts misunderstood as attempts at conversion.

(7) As neighborhoods become heterogeneous and the values of the dominant group become threatened, there is the tendency for such a group to withdraw. Some go to the suburbs. Others use voluntary associations as refuges in which to evade meaningful encounters with those of other races. Among these voluntary associations, the church has perhaps become the most respectable "escape" in America. It is not possible to equate such withdrawals or evasions with the moral and intellectual demands of the present Space Age of which we are a part. Suburban communities likewise attempt to shield themselves from newcomers whom they consider to be a threat. Not only are Negroes, but others of different heritages, excluded from certain communities. In this regard, Jesus Christ —himself a Jew—would not be a welcome citizen of communities such as Grosse Pointe, Michigan, or Bronxville, New York. This attempt to escape responsibilities relates again to the problems of involvement and basic values. Studies indi-

cate that the vast majority of the middle class group in an average community will attempt to sit on the side lines when controversy arises and not implicate themselves unless forced to do so. In fact, one of the most difficult problems in inter-group relations is how to maneuver such groups into positions where they must take a stand on controversial issues. This was the major issue in Little Rock, and it is the greater issue in the race relations of the average community. Tumin's study of Gaston County, North Carolina, indicated clearly that there was a small group of whites which was very much opposed to integration and a comparable group which was very much in favor. The vast middle group, however, was not about to get involved if it could avoid it.

It is easier to move on to the suburb or hide in the church than it is to come to meaningful confrontation with differences, and make one's influence felt in the processes of conflict through which new relationships are forged.

(8) Most communities in change feel that such change downgrades them. This is particularly true of suburban neigh-borhoods. Almost invariably the first settlers have more status than do the newcomers. A consideration of almost any well-known suburb such as Scarsdale, New York, Shaker Heights, Ohio, or Westport, Connecticut, reveals that when the Jews arrive, the neighborhood considers itself to be starting a down-hill slide. When the Negroes come, they are positive of it. In past years the same arguments were used concerning those of Irish, Italian or Polish backgrounds.

The core problem of the discriminatory aspects of race rela-tions would seem to be contained in a single popular word—"snootiness." It is agreed that a community without a status ordering would flounder in dealing with its problems. However, this agreement leads us to pose the pertinent question, "What are the criteria for status in America?" We should examine such pedestrian values as implied by length of residence in a given community, religious affiliation, racial background or social class, and ask ourselves if service to a community should not be the real measure of worth. The substitution of service for "snootiness" could immeasurably enrich the lives of all community members, both those with deep roots in its affairs and those who have had time to grow only tap roots.

(9) The next of the issues posed is that of power. Most communities in change go through a power fight. In this writer's judgment this aspect of American life has been neglected. Could not evidence be gathered to support the hypothesis that it is impossible for a youth who is a member of a group which is powerless in a community to mature? Would he, in fact, experience some trauma to his individuality because of the anomalous position of his group in the community? Without power one feels himself of little worth. One of the great attractions of our religion is that it teaches the humblest that he has power because he is a child of God. Hence, regardless of how impotent he is otherwise, there is some self-respect left. However, Adler's theory that people who feel compromised in their potency tend to overcompensate by aggression in order to overcome their limitations is, perhaps, only half correct. They also resign in apathy. The class apathy of the slum-dwellers today is mute testimony to the powerlessness they feel.

It would not be hard to make a case that the great advances in race relations within the past two decades are not due to what we have done in the intergroup and religious fields, but rather due to the fact that Negroes have moved from the South and now hold a political balance of power in those states which rank high in Negro inhabitants. These are states in which the two political parties are about evenly divided and are key states in political elections. Hence the minority group holds veto power over who is going to capture and hold office. This is one way of securing leverages to power. Law is another. The great legal decisions have also shored up civil rights. They have strengthened the recognition of the change of power relations within the groups. If one believes, however, that people's rights are respected merely because they are human beings, but without power, he should look at the sad state of the migrant laborers. Without power, i.e., without the ballot, they are exploited and pushed from pillar to post. Residence laws discriminate against them in securing relief and harassment of them almost becomes the norm. Newburgh, New York, is perhaps the outstanding symbol of this in the North. Numerous evidences of it abound in the Southwest and West.

It has already been indicated that the domniant group in a community tries to work through integrative processes. This integrative approach to the powerless in the past has been aimed at the more intelligent, alienating them in their sentiments and sympathies from the groups of which they were a part, getting them to take stock in the great mythologies of the American Dream, and making them ashamed of their heritage. Ultimately they were to be transmuted into so-called Ideal Americans. This means the constant siphoning off of the bright ones, still leaving the residual group to stew in its own problems. Slums are a monument to this kind of action. They stand as an institutionalized part of every great American city.

As another evidence of our great humanitarian motivations, we have moved out both at home and abroad to serve certain populations, reasoning that if they were sufficiently served in Egypt, as it were, they would not launch out in search of a Promised Land. But service creates dependency, and is in fact a tranquilizer. The great outpouring of service here and abroad is a dominant power group's way of trying to hold tenable its position, and at the same time indoctrinate the world with its value system.

With these vast concentrations of marginal population in the inner cities of the megalopolises, we are fast approaching the situation faced by many past civilizations. Today, there are estimated to be a million more people living in the city slums of America than on all of its farms. There are estimated to be a million more marginal people on farms who may yet migrate. Past civilizations found it easier to keep these marginal people amused rather than to integrate them purposively into the common life of their society. The lesson of history should be illuminating to us. Such attrition of resources brought about their downfall. Our future is yet to be determined.

Integration into the common life of the community is different for the Negro and certain of the Spanish-speaking population than it was for past groups which have already been assimilated into American life. The difference is by color. When the intelligent Negro youth is caught up in these processes and is transmuted, his limits are still circumscribed, because his color stands out as a badge of identity. He finds himself rejected because of the way he looks, not because of what he is. For him other measures must be employed to take the place of this integrative process. One effective substitute lies in the process of taking power. It should be remembered that power *has* to be taken. It cannot be bestowed. When the powerless take power, conflict is inevitable. This is anathema to most religiously oriented people. Most of them believe that religion and love go together and that conflict is something evil. They find themselves to be ambivalent. They would like to see the "little man" succeed, yet they fear the threat to their own preferential position if too much power is wrested from them.

The church is remiss in not making more demonstrable the fact that there is power in moral position, if based on thoughtful premises, as well as in being a human being. Church-related people could find true spiritual satisfactions in observing and being a part of this process. There is nothing more exhilarating than to see people taking the first fumbling steps toward freedom; they are reaffirming one of our greatest faiths, namely, that all men cherish freedom and chafe under oppression. To witness groups taking power and forcing vested interests to take into account minority voices in communal decision-making is to watch democracy working at its best. Yet, most of us stand in the middle of such goodness and do not attempt to comprehend it. Some feel threatened, so oppose it.

(10) Most communities in change are characterized by a high degree of physical mobility. One inner-city public elementary school known to this author must enroll 106 children for every initial 100 on the roll in order to keep a constant enrollment. Yet most agencies, including the church, operate programs for children and migrants in general, as if they were stable populations.

III. Some Things to Do

At the expense of being misunderstood, it seems worth mentioning some efforts which dedicated people could make in meeting the challenges of changing communities. The following are suggested:

(1) The church must continue to try to bring society to judgment on this issue of racism. It is man's most dangerous myth. Sciences and morality are converging in their agreement

that no one race of the world has a superior capacity. Or stated more positively, "All groups have the capacities to become what any present group now is." From a spiritual point of view, the imperative is the recognition that all men are brothers, and not that one group constitutes a threat to another.

This issue is pertinent not only to the problems of Negro-White or Oriental-Occidental. It includes theories of race which can be applied to whomever one decides to dislike, as Hitler demonstrated. In this regard Christians need to concern themselves more with this curious thread of anti-Semitism which runs like a low-grade infection in the body politic. It reappears every time stress occurs and resistance is lowered. Where in our religion is this damnable virus carried? How can it be eliminated? Concern about the ideology of race should be a supreme anxiety to all religious denominations.

(2) Show interest in the well-being of newcomers for reasons other than to entice them to join a particular fellowship. Every professing Christian, supposedly, is under obligation to witness to the faith within him. How that faith is interpreted, however, can make a large difference. "Rice Christians" have demonstrated the inherent difficulties when people are made to compromise their values in order to receive assistance from others.

(3) Help congregations re-examine their prejudices. When communities are in change all members are brought to significant confrontation. This is a teachable moment. It is the time when interpretation can have the most meaning. There is little value in having nice study groups about race in middle class suburban ghettos which are "lily white." Values really

emerge when a community is in conflict. Opportunities, even though they may be pregnant with discord, should be welcomed as touchstones to test the validity of our committments. Will they prove to be of sufficient worth to produce fellowship across the lines of difference?

(4) Try to strengthen the civil rights of all. One of the great undertakings facing our society is that of the completion of undergirding the so-called human rights with civil law, in this way creating stronger civil rights. Civil rights are admittedly only the first mile, the forced mile, in intergroup relations. It is the necessary first step, however.

(5) Intervene in neighborhood panic. Many fine things have been done by different groups to try to prepare communities for change. Some undoubtedly have had a gainful impact. Many are of the belief, however, that it is impossible to prepare a community for change. Nothing significant happens until the community is significantly confronted. Some groups have been effective in allaying the panic which has played a community into the clutches of the blockbuster real estate sharks. Every congregation can inform itself as to progressions through which communities go when they are in the throes of confrontation, and prepare itself for the eventuality when it comes home to them.

(6) The majority of communities have not been integrated by great petitions and consensus of large bodies, but rather by a small action group—the Gideon's dozen. One does not need the consensus of a large group to desegregate a community. All he needs is to find someone who wishes to sell his house and is willing to sell it to a Negro family, someone else who is Negro who wishes to buy, and the money with which to

finance the deal. It is unrealistic to expect large bodies such as church congregations to make significant moves through consensus. The most that dedicated members can hope for is autonomy enough within the fellowship to act as described above, without ostracism from the fellowship.

(7) Fight anomie. A significant aspect of the community in change is that the norms of behavior become blurred and equivocal. The controls of the old group are wavering and those of the new have not yet been established. The church has no more significant role than that of "shoring up" the perimeters of authority, in order that the youth of the community may at all times have a clear perspective of the norms. Surely this is a place where all religious groups have more in common than there are differences among them. The changing community, and especially the one in the inner city, is generally the older community. New groups with their differing population of children to be educated, their lower economic status, which frequently produces the greatest demands upon the communal facilities, find themselves taking second best. If people are ever to learn to live together amicably, it is going to be in these mixed neighborhoods. Yet it is precisely here that there is the tendency to have the poorest facilities available to make this satisfactory social compound. In such areas are found the oldest schools, the least able teachers (the novitiates and superannuates), antiquated street lighting, the fewest police per capita and spasmodic garbage collection. It is as if the city fathers anticipate a change to lower socio-economic status and consequently prod the neighborhood along the road to its prophetic destiny.

How to keep firm, clear and unequivocal images of what the perimeters of authority are in a changing community is one of our chief challenges.

(8) Emphasize more social action to complement service.

In our era of conformity this is not easy. Social science, in recent years, has come to the realization that one cannot separate personality from social structure. One of the most neglected aspects of social development is that we have preoccupied ourselves with the changing personality of mankind and have not spent adequate time changing his afferent structures. It may be more important to help an individual get out of a slum than it is to serve him in a slum. It is more useful to help the minority person get a job than it is to provide him with relief. It is more germaine to make certain that the child of minority people can use all public facilities than it is to provide counselors to "tinker with their psyches" in order to remove the trauma to self-perception stemming from powerlessness. It may be more important to break up *de facto* school segregation than it is to have more special services in the schools. All these are social action jobs. They are not challenges of service in any traditional way. This the church must recognize and make proper provisions for.

IV. *The Prospect*

In the years ahead, the Church is to be confronted as at few times in her history. The issue is whether she is dynamic enough to hurdle the barriers of race and social class in order to effectively bind this nation together in one spiritual community; or whether, lacking such impetus, these masses who are now congregating in our cities, who are rejected because of class and race, will despair that such identities can ever be achieved and turn to other ideologies. Already the Black Muslims have told them that the Christian philosophy of love, forbearance and patience provides the rationale for their servitude. Now churches have the choice of either bringing their memberships to judgment on these aforementioned issues or being brought to judgment themselves by a world segment anxious for definitive action. Changing communities offer concrete testing grounds for such action.

The Responsibility of Church and Synagogue as Institutions in the Community

VERY REV. MSGR. JOHN J. EGAN

If there is one underlying theme which unites Catholics, Protestants, and Jews, it is the belief in a personal God to whom we all have the obligation to give witness; and in the essentially related belief that all men, as special creatures of God, possess a unique dignity by virtue of their creation. This notion of kinship in God is so deeply embedded in the tradition of all our faiths that it cannot be rejected without at the same time rejecting our place in the community of the Judaeo-Christian faithful.

It is precisely this aspect of the Judaeo-Christian tradition which has been under persistent and successful attack for well over a century.

Undoubtedly the most spectacular of the attacks was launched by Marx and Engel. The infamous dictum that "religion is the opiate of the people" is well expressed in the totalitarian systems which explicitly reject unique individual dignity and which relate the entire meaning of the individual to the progress of society.

Yet if the dialectic of *Das Kapital* is the most spectacular rejection of the kinship in God, it is for the American scene at least, probably not the most significant.

In actual practice *Das Kapital* utilized a view of the nature of man which took a different form, but the same substance, in the Anglo-American philosophy of Herbert Spencer and William Graham Sumner. Spencerian philosophy enjoys the distinction of being the most pervading and enduring of all the philosophies of man ever proposed on the American continent. It is, indeed, so pervading that it has influenced, subtly but effectively, the Judaeo-Christian tradition in America. And that is the source of our difficulty.

What is this Spencerian view? Drawing an analogy from the purely biological findings of Darwin, the English philosopher, Herbert Spencer, in a series of volumes entitled *Synthetic Philosophy* published in the early 1860's, proposed that man is a social organism in evolutionary process toward perfection; and that at the social level, the same processes of natural selection are in play as Darwin found in the biological world. Man evolves toward a more perfect strain as the unfit, the misfits, and the weak die off from their lack of competitive ability. And, Spencer holds, this is good. The weak die off so that the race becomes perfected. It is their function in life; and if we interfere with the process, or permit the weak to live and breed, we merely impede the progress of society.[1]

Spencer's thesis, which came to be known as Social Darwinism, was popularized on the American scene by the prolific William Graham Sumner. His own words are quite succinct:

> Many . . . are frightened at liberty, especially under the form of competition, which they elevate into a bugbear. They think it bears harshly on the weak. They do not perceive that here "the strong" and "the weak" are terms which admit of no definition unless they are made equivalent to the industrious and the idle, the frugal and the extravagant. They do not perceive, furthermore, that if we do not

like the survival of the fittest, we have only one possible alternative, and that is the survival of the unfittest. The former is the law of civilization; the latter is the law of decay.[2]

With hindsight, it is easy to see that the Spencerian dictum and the dictum of *Das Kapital* are remarkably similar. In each, the individual is meaningless except as he serves as a cog in the perfection of the race. The specific difference between Marx and Spencer is that the former rejected capitalism and free enterprise; while the latter provided a most accommodating rationale for its abuses.

As a coherent theory, Social Darwinism was discredited in the cataclysm of the Great Depression. But it has never been completely rejected in the American ethos. As late as World War II, for instance, textbooks being used at the Harvard School of Business were direct and detailed interpretations of Spencer's thesis. Most of the present leaders of the American business community were educated in a system which explicitly taught the Spencerian thesis as the ultimate philosophical rationale for the free enterprise system.

It is, however, a deteriorating point of view. As a coherent philosophy, it need not overly concern us. But its residual effects on American society bear a direct relationship to the problem of race relations.

The most obvious of these residual effects is in our attitude toward the poor. Americans admit, if grudgingly and with one eye on the tax bill, that it is a good thing to give aid to the deserving poor—to those who through no fault of their own are unable to make their way in society. But the emphasis is on "deserving." The man who will not work, or the man whose personality apparatus prevents him from being competitive, or the lazy man, or the shiftless man, is not deserving of our help. If we must help him in order to keep him from practicing violence against the good order of the state, at least we need keep him no more than alive and submissive.

This habitual distinction between the "deserving" poor and the "unfit" poor is the most compelling evidence that we do not really implement our primal religious belief in the God-related diginity of man. We are still dominated by the Spencerian dictum that man is worthy of our attention only as he actively contributes to society; only as he has a utilitarian purpose.

Thus, while our American ethos gives lip service to the notion of the dignity of man, the practical customs by which a society implements its ethos deny this notion. The apparent contradiction between our juridical assent to the rights of man and our treatment of minorities is more easily understood against this background. In reality, our allegiance to the rights of man is juridical only. It has not been accompanied by the only concept which gives it meaning and ultimate rationality: Kinship in God.

For both history and logic compel us to believe that unique individual dignity is inconceivable except as the individual relates to the Judaeo-Christian God. The Greek city-state of Aristotle and Plato gave us perhaps the highest expression of a civilization ordered outside the framework of God the Father.

Yet Aristotle's concept of the poor is not far different from that of Spencer. Extreme poverty, Aristotle holds, "lowers the character of a democracy" and therefore the poor should be given means to help themselves. But let the help be only in the form of means to better themselves. If the poor do not better themselves, then aid to them is wasteful.[3]

Historically, it is in the Jewish and Christian tradition that the poor possess a dignity which rises above their utility and the good order of society—precisely because their dignity, as well as the dignity of all, is based upon a relationship with God that transcends the proximate purposes of society.

Thus it is the specific mission of the churches and synagogues to infuse into our society that understanding of the unique dignity of each man which comes from his status as a creature of God—a dignity so unique that he deserves our personal commitment whether he be rich or poor; a dignity so unique that, if poor, he deserves our help whether he be ambitious or lazy, moral or immoral, grateful or belligerent; a dignity so unique that he deserves our understanding regardless of his skin, his temperament, or his cultural traditions.

For there is a direct and vital relationship between the problem of dignity in God and the problem of race relations. As there is no intelligible basis for aiding the poor and unfit outside of the concept of a God who is Father, there is no intelligible basis for racial tolerance outside of the concept of God who is Father. Given the assumption that there is no God of Israel, that men are left to their own devices, both the extinction of a race and the extinction of the poor are rational, economical, and humanitarian approaches to the perfectability of man. Hitler was no less rational than Spencer; and neither was less rational than the rabid southern (or northern) racist. All either explicitly or implicitly reject the fundamental basis of belief in the God of Israel.

I have examined the problem of our attitude toward the poor, not only because it illustrates the gap in our mores of individual dignity (upon which any sound race relations must be built), but also because, in the present crisis, the poor and the racial minorities are often and extensively identified with each other. Or perhaps in a larger sense, the question of wealth and poverty has been intertwined with all minority relations in America. All immigrant groups, all minority groups, in America, have been at first poor. To be at once poor and a minority has been the lot of all our "strangers in the land," as the studies of John Higham and Oscar Handlin demonstrate.[4] It has not been an easy lot. Historically, American antipathies toward the poor have blended with American antipathies toward minorities, and the stereotype still prevails. Indeed, once an immigrant group has ceased to be predominantly poor, it has ceased to be regarded as a minority in the general American consciousness. Thus, although residual and often painful prejudices still work against Catholics and Jews, the public consciousness does not place them in the same minority category as Negroes, Southern Whites, Puerto Ricans, and Mexicans.

This intertwining of identification (and hostility) towards the poor and towards minorities has profound implications for contemporary race relations.

For it is all too easy for the latent racist to rationalize his hostility toward minorities on the basis of their poverty. It is all too easy to ask, "Why don't they help themselves?" It is all too easy to assume, with Spencer, that the Negro (for instance) is poor; and poor because lazy; and because lazy, not worthy of concern.

While on the one hand we argue for racial tolerance on the ground that all men are creatures of God and thus possessed of their unique dignity, we permit ourselves to apply Spencer's test of fitness to the poor. We thus perpetuate a moral double standard which is not lost to our people. We cannot expect to be taken seriously on the question of race relations if we do not insist on being taken seriously on the question of the poor. The point is that we will never be successful in eliminating the cancer of racial intolerance from our society until we also eliminate the cancer of intolerance of the poor.

In the next two days we need to keep clearly in mind that whatever educative value our institutional practises take on—whether they be primary, as in the case of our educational forms, or secondary, as in the case of the example of our administrative actions—their image must reflect the totality of our belief in the dignity of man—a dignity which extends to the poor as well as to the minority; a dignity which does not ask, "What good are you?" or "What are you?" but a dignity which asks, in fact, no question at all.

We must keep clearly in mind that race relations rest on the same basis as all other human relations: the notion of man's dignity in God. When we practice unjust wage policies we violate the same principle as when we practice discriminatory hiring policies. When we gear our welfare institutions to serve predominantly the middle class we repudiate human dignity as much as when we restrict our welfare programs according to race. When we approve, in our educational schema, the moral status of wealth, we display the same contempt for the creatures of God as we do when we approve the teaching of theories of racial inferiority. What is more important, we must keep clearly in mind that love of neighbor, love, especially of the poor, is neither an intellectual position nor an elevating sentiment. It is an action. Here Martin Buber's insight is compelling, and I quote:

> The Bible knows that it is impossible to command the love of man. I am incapable of feeling love toward every man, although God Himself command me. The Bible does not directly enjoin the love of man, but by using the dative puts it rather in the form of an *act* of love. (I must love "to Him.")[5]

Love of the poor, then, rests on Buber's dative. It is an act. The Sacred Books abound with concrete injunctions to feed the hungry, clothe the naked, do kindness to the stranger, comfort the brethren. Why? God answers: "What if he cries for redress, and I, the ever merciful, listen to him?" (Exod. 22:25). "Remember what God you worship." (Lev. 19:9-10). Love of the poor is an act; it is enjoyable because we are all of God, and God is the God of all.

If then, love of the poor is the open manifestation of man's dignity in God; and if love of the poor is in the first instance an act of dative—it necessarily implies involvement. An essential element of love, of charity, of almsgiving, of the giving of comfort, is an empathy that can come only from involvement and identification. God calls upon his people to love by recalling to their minds their own historical experience: "You were alien once, in the Land of Egypt" (Lev. 19:34); "Do not forget that thou wast once a slave in Egypt" (Deut. 24:19)—injunctions that are directed as much to the Christian as to the Hebrew community.

Love of the poor, as a matter of fact, is related to human dignity only insofar as it involves empathy. Then, says Leo XIII, "It neither connotes pride in the giver nor inflicts shame on the one who receives. The disposition to ask assistance from others with confidence, and to grant it with kindness, is part of our very nature."[6]

The spirit of empathy and understanding, the reverence for human dignity, which is an essential part of charity and love for the poor, is a value in itself: one of the prime sources of human enrichment, and a marvelous example of the way in which Divine Providence draws good out of evil. For the spirit of empathy implied in a true love of the poor, as Pope Pius XI points out in a memorable passage, goes far beyond the simple alleviation of physical want:

> But even though a state of things be pictured in which every man receives at last all that is his due, a wide field will nevertheless remain open for charity. For justice alone, even though most faithfully observed, can remove indeed the cause of social strife, but can never bring about a union of hearts and minds. Yet this union, binding men together, is the main principle of stability in all institutions, no matter how perfect they may seem, which aim at establishing social peace and promoting mutual aid.[7]

Thus it is necessary not only to reshape our attitudes toward the notion of poverty, but to regear our involvement with the poor. We have had sufficient conversation about the dignity of man; what is required of us, as religious institutions, is to become involved with the man whose dignity we preach.

We need to ask ourselves whether our institutions have abandoned the poor, both formally and symbolically. Do we seek energetically to find the poor? To serve them? To become one with them? Or are we, as institutions, becoming as middle-class as the majority of our people?

Moreover, our institutions must be concerned not only with the people they formally serve, but also with the neighborhoods in which they are located. For a church, a synagogue, a school, or a hospital is not merely an institution—it is a religious institution. It is a symbol—an image, if you will—of religion and of God. The religious institution which remains aloof from its neighborhood, and whose administrators do not involve themselves with the aspirations, causes, and organizations of the neighborhood, are by virtue of their symbolic role denying God in that neighborhood. This is as true of an orphanage, for instance, which does not normally serve the immediate neighborhood, as it is true of a settlement house.

Finally, we need to beware of the trap of putting religion in the role of a tool toward better race relations. As religious men, we reject racial intolerance not primarily because we are useful in removing it, but because it is a denial of the God of Israel. It is the people of God who alone bear the responsibility for racial intolerance. This is an awesome responsibility. Neither the Jew nor the Christian can escape it. He can only fulfill it, or fail at it; and failing at it, he bears false witness not only to his neighbor, but to God.

NOTES

1. For a thorough discussion of the impact of the Spencerian thesis on America, see Richard Hofstadter, *Social Darwinism in American Thought* (American Historical Association, 1944); also available in a revised paperback edition: Beacon Press, 1955. For a trenchant criticism of Spencerian views by a native American philosopher who was hardly in the tradition of conservative theology, see "Lecture One" in William James, *Pragmatism* (Meridian Books edition, 1955), esp. p. 24 ff.
2. *Essays*, II, 56, cited in Hofstadter, *ibid.* (Beacon Press edition), p. 57.
3. *Politics*, Bk. VI, Ch. 5 (1320a, 28-40).
4. John Higham, *Strangers in the Land* (Rutgers University Press, 1955). Oscar Handlin, *The Uprooted* (Atlantic—Little Brown, 1951).
5. Martin Buber, essay on "Herman Cohen," *The Writings of Martin Buber*, ed. Will Herberg (Meridian Books, 1956), p. 103.
6. Leo XIII, encyclical letter "Christian Democracy" (Graves de Communi), Jan. 13, 1901, par. 16, Paulist Press edition.
7. Pius XI, encyclical letter, "Reconstructing the Social Order," (Quadragesimo Anno), May 15, 1931, p. 137, America Press edition.

Relation of Church and Synagogue to Other Community Forces

Rabbi Morris Adler

The theme of this paper deals with several of the new dimensions of tension and dilemma in which organized religion finds itself involved, as it seeks to sustain itself in a free and pluralistic society. To be sure tension is nothing new to religion. It may even be said to be the condition most congenial to its growth and vitality. Tensions inhere in religion and stimulate that dynamism of restless quest which its most creative spirits reflect. The peace that is sometimes spoken of as the harbor and goal of religious striving is marked neither by quiescence nor inertness. It is rather a glimpse into or a calming recognition of an effulgent wholeness which embraces without resolving the polarities of religion's tensions.

When the prophet described himself as a "man of strife and a man of contention to the whole earth," he was referring to his relations with his contemporaries. His words, however, describe just as truly the inner stresses under which the man of religion lives, and help to suggest the fierce inquietude which subsisted at the center of the prophet's life. The Talmud observes that the man of religious feeling and learning will experience rest neither in this world nor in the world beyond. Immortality

101

would be a doubtful boon were it merely to substitute for physical death, that inert tranquility which approaches spiritual death. The incessant and futile attempt to bridge the unbridgeable, absolute gap between God and man; the agonizing yearning for the divine, a yearning which can never know fulfillment or satiety; the inexpressible that one senses which cannot be communicated and yet clamors for expression; the contrasting claims of reason and faith; the universal out-reaching midst the embodiments of one's tradition in numerous particularities; the eternity that knocks at the windowpanes of the moment one occupies in history; the consciousness of one's mortality coupled with one's hunger for everlasting life; the ultimates to which religion bids us raise our eyes and the urgencies which crowd us at every move; the grace of inherited forms and the creative need for the freshness of new responses—these constitute part of that unceasing inquietude which the religious enterprise stimulates.

A faith which seeks to dissolve this perpetual restlessness by eliminating one or another of the elements in tension not alone shallows the deeps and reduces the intensity of the religious experience, but also may be said to pervert it. The opposing elements in the tension are needed for the completeness of a faith which aims to embrace all of life as well as for the correction of any tendency to an exclusive emphasis which would do violence to the multifaceted character of human needs and capacities, for, as Emerson said in another connection, while each is a great half, it might be an impossible whole. These dilemmas integral to the nature of the genuine religious experience are increased, as we have said, in the case of religious bodies functioning in a democratic order. The three new stresses to which we will here make reference are implied in three divisions of the subject, namely, the relation of religion to voluntary groups in society, relationships between religious groups, and lastly, relationships on the part of religious groups to government and political forces.

Religion in our free society is surrounded by a secularity which dominates substantial areas of that society. No longer is church or synagogue set in a climate of universal acceptance of fundamental religious attitudes and beliefs. However the religious of Western civilization differed among themselves, they were in agreement upon such basic ideas as the existence of God, Whose Will governs the world and Whose reality is the foundation of all moral law; the divine imprint which gives man his most authentic character; the unity of mankind which in the long run is more decisive than the conflicts and divisiveness which now fragmentize it; the moral purpose underlying the social order. The authority of religion, at least in the realm of theory, informed society, however far behind that theory it habitually lagged in practice. This condition persisted till modern times. But then there "arose a new king . . . who knew not Joseph," and religion was removed from its social predominance. The assumptions of religion are not explicit or acknowledged in the cultural and intellectual life outside of it. Its views of life and of man are no longer the common heritage of society. Man has, as Joseph Wood Krutch expresses it in his *The Modern Temper*, "put off his royal robes." The temper of modern life is secular. This secularity is not so much an ideology as a fact; not so much a rationale as a force, enabling America to be at once, as Reinhold Niebuhr points out, both secular and pious.

We are not here dealing with a secularism which is a philosophically organized denial of religious premises and concepts and which functions in the life of its faithful as a religion of anti-religion. The secularity we have reference to is the product of a complex of historic factors which have united to bring the modern period into being and which have helped shape it. It is the common ground of those who are members of one of the diverse religious creeds of our society and those who are affiliated with none. It is independent, certainly in its palpable and overt forms of religious motivations and imperatives. It does not take the position of embattled repudiation or explicit denial. It is neutral not because its believes in the equal validity of the options of religion and non-religion, but because it does not invoke either the forms or doctrines of faith. Many of the most influential centers of power and authority in a free society operate in just such an atmosphere of neutrality, in which religion as a recognized and affirmed commitment is wholly absent. One may trace streams of religious influence that, in greater or lesser measure, have entered these institutions of secularity, but these streams now flow on such a deep subterranean level that they go unobserved even by those who are the beneficiaries of their enriching impact. Such powerful and indispensable agencies as government, the press, public education, industry, labor are instances of a secularity which in their essentials do not reflect a religious character.

The dilemma is bold and vivid. Religion which seeks to interpenetrate all of life with its truths and values must not only do its work in an area apparently unclaimed by religious commitment, but must relate itself negatively or positively to a wide-ranging secularity. The dilemma is whether it should turn its back upon this broad arena of human interest and endeavor and read itself out of the crucial and powerful centers of effectiveness or should it cooperate with the secular arms of society and run the risk by such cooperation of implying that religion is not a prime necessity for the performance of good acts and the promotion of moral policies.

A second dilemma born of the new circumstances of modern life is that raised by the presence of many differing religions in a free society. Religions as we have known them in the Western world are the bearers of an absolute idea. They view themselves as charting *the way* to salvation, the secret of which has been entrusted to them alone. They address themselves to the ultimate questions of life with such an inflexible intensity of conviction about the validity of their answers as to confer upon them unduplicated singularity. Absolute truths are after all non-negotiable and he who holds to them, limits the area of dialogue and denies a basis of parity. Contending absolutes leave no room for mutual accommodation. Yet the sovereign facts of life in a free society force upon religion the inescapable necessity of recognizing *de facto* if not *de jure* the presence of other creeds with equally insistent claims to authority and absoluteness. To fuse one's convictions of theological exclusiveness with the practice of a broad social inclusiveness touching other religious orientations represents a new challenge for which the historic experience of the faiths of the Western world has not prepared him. The contingencies of past history have either allowed them to be dominant and established in a given period or subordinate and suppressed. They have not had the opportunity (would any say "the misfortune"?) of living on a basis of social equality with other faiths. How does one resolve a dilemma, one of the horns of which is a theory of absolute right and the other an interaction which in conferring equality on many faiths implies or seems to imply the relativity of each of them?

A third dilemma is crystallized by the tripartite formulation of our subject. How does religion relate itself to government and the political life in a free society: For in a democracy, government is not a Caesar apart from and over us, but a collectivity of which we are a constituent. However imperfectly the political machinery serves as an instrument of "we the people," there is present a corrective for the perversion of the power that belongs to the people, and this constitutes a distinguishing characteristic of the free society.

But in more immediate ways we are involved in the work

and activity of government. Government today not alone reaches into those areas in which it gives political and social expression to values long cherished by religion (such as human welfare, human dignity, peace, equality, justice), but also by its pervasiveness colors the entire climate of society. Government today is far more than a political instrumentality. It helps give unity and direction to the group-life of its people and indeed in many instances to their life as individuals.

What should be the relation of religion to the political life of its times? This is not an identical problem with that suggested by the terms Church and State. American tradition and law oppose the harnessing in any formal way of the machinery with the institutions of religion or with the public or private exercise of religion by an adherent of religion. This does not mean the removal of religion from the public domain. For religion is more than a cult, an agency, an institution. Its unrestricted scope is suggested by the comment of Dr. William Temple, the late Archbishop of Canterbury, that "it is a great mistake to suppose that God is only or even mainly concerned with religion." Religion is a system of concepts about life and the nature of man—a complex of sensitivities, a bearer of a divine mandate and a fellowship of men dedicated to a purpose in history and beyond history. It places or should place these ideas and purposes above its institutional interests and concerns. This dynamic purposefulness will not permit it to insulate itself behind the ramparts of its formalism and stay aloof from the currents of our time. Yet to enter these currents exposes it to many hazards. There is a degree of involvement beyond which it may not venture, since in its entanglement with the immediacies it may become estranged from ultimates. Politics by its very nature is concerned with expendiencies, with the possible rather than the good, the urgent rather than the important, the popular rather than the ideal. Prudence and compromise are attributes of political life, and not improperly so. Can religion enter the political realm and not be infected by that which, though it is acceptable and even proper in political action, is fatal when absorbed into the religious life? If religion is to be effective, it must be involved. If it becomes involved, it may cease to be religion and become yet another pressure group. Here we have the third of the dilemmas which our subject highlights.

A detailed program is beyond the scope of this paper. We limit ourselves to some of the cautions and restraints which should guide religion as it enters the public arena in which voluntary secular organizations and the government function and as it relates itself to other faiths, impelled as it is by an earnest desire to advance in some degree in contemporary social life the purposes which it projects for all history and all mankind.

For involve itself, religion must, else it will remain neutral in crucial areas which so desperately need something of its passion, perspective and purpose and will become increasingly irrelevant in an age aquiver with apprehension and confounded by perplexity. It may mean abandoning society to haphazard influences of social circumstance and political contingency. It may have an even worse consequence in that its abdication may contribute to the development of a civic religion which by the standards of the Judeo-Christian tradition can only be accounted as a modern idolatry.

It can be maintained with much force that no society is secular. Every society inherits or fashions a religion. A non-religionist like John Dewey speaks of "A Common Faith" emerging out of the structure and pursuits of American society. Its forms are presently borrowed from the dominant Christian faiths in our country. But even as it appropriates these forms it is disassociating them from their original traditional context of ideas and values. What is happening to Christmas is only the most dramatic symptom of an entire process. Between the invocations with which we begin and the benedictions with which we close many of our public functions, the sessions of Congress and the legislatures of our several states, are programs of activities which are untouched by the religious frame in which they are formally set. They are basically non-religious in substance and quality despite their obeisance to a religious form.

Where the ultimates are business or the state or an economic system or a political party or any phase of life which true religion views as relative, the end result must be idolatry. The civic religion of the Roman empire was the worship of the Roman emperor. While a civic religion need not become embodied in a state or an established church, it must perforce lead to a deification of the collective purposes, ideals and other relativities of its society and its age. In a transitional period, since symbols are not easily improvised, the civic religion may lean for these on the historic religions. The content of the Judeo-Christian tradition becomes muted, even though its external forms are stressed and imposed upon public life. It becomes more important to put up a creche in a public place than to teach and interpret the doctrine of Incarnation. It seems to be a paradox, yet it is nonetheless sober fact, that the multiplication of prayers and observances taken into our public life from historic religions may represent both a dilution of and a substitution for the religions from which they were adopted. Unheralded are the doctrines which give substance and meaning to the forms. Eliminated are the deeply rooted particularities of experience, belief and mood which give to religious expression its passion and vitality.

Hence I believe it to be of singular importance that the historic religious traditions of America enjoy high visibility on the scene of America's social strivings, struggles and planning. The effect as I see it will be twofold. First it will check the growth of a civic non-denominational, non-traditional religion which must inevitably culminate in a national idolatry. Secondly, I believe that it will reinforce the effort to establish racial justice, for example, with an authority and an impetus no non-religious institution can equal. One of the painful ironies of our time is that religion, whose social concerns flow from deep sources of belief and commitment, has not been in the vanguard of the fight for racial justice. A few years ago, Dean Liston Pope of the Yale University Divinity School spoke these words, "The Church has lagged behind the Supreme Court as the conscience of the nation on the question of race and it has fallen far behind trade unions, factories, schools, department stores, athletic gatherings and most other major human associations, as far as the achievement of integration in its own life is concerned."

Even the adherents of religion often feel that it is necessary to work through secular agencies to achieve desirable social goals since their own Church organizations have either contented themselves with innocuous pronouncements or have not evidenced any concern at all. Religion should welcome the support of every secular group whose motivations are sincere and whose social goals coincide with its own. There is a profound sense in which nothing human is secular. But even as religion enters into such a partnership, it should not relinquish its role as a critic, since in perspective and purpose it ranges far beyond the immediate goals. For religion, the achievement of racial justice is not an element in a foreign policy, a factor making for a good image abroad; or the fulfillment of the implications of a political system or doctrine, nor yet the price for domestic tranquillity. It represents an objective transcending all these. It is part of a program that is grounded in a cosmic scheme of things, arising out of a mandate of God to man. It should impart to its partnership with secular agencies the assurance and the compelling power of a divine imperative which animates the believer.

Recognizing a judgment above and beyond history, religion can deepen our social programs with the vision and insight that derive from it. Religion's solicitude embraces not only the victim of racial injustice but also its perpetrator. It can thus without sacrificing intensity and resolve help make our social struggle one that not only combats evil but upholds and articulates the larger good. Religion can focus upon the social scene the wholeness which Martin Buber intimated is lacking when he said, "Individualism understands only a part of man, collectivism understands man only as a part. Individualism sees man only in relation to himself—but collectivism does not see man at all; it sees society." Religion by working alongside of secular agencies devoted to racial justice need not be reduced to the status of an agency or a social work program, as long as it holds before it the high sights of its own purpose and nature. Religion is more widely professed than respected among us. Can it truly hope for the respect of modern men if it affirms in rhetoric the dignity of man and is blind in fact to the misery of man? If there are dangers to religion in its alliance with the variety of secular agencies working in the field of racial justice, it seems to me there is greater danger to it if it refrains from such cooperation.

Religion however must be armed not only with resolve and faith but what may be equally essential in this context—the rich and sovereign quality of humility. William Temple once remarked that on some social questions religious people have no more reliable judgment than atheists. There are technical matters involving the knowledge of facts for which faith, however pure and lofty, cannot be a substitute. Religion must therefore realize its limitations and speak with proper diffidence on many occasions. It must not throw the full weight of its claims and prestige to a detail of a program which was in all likelihood not contained in any divine revelation which it enjoyed. Religion is often likely to win a degree of respect for its reserve that it could never win by any pretension to undeserved authority or omniscience.

We have alluded to the dilemma with which the diversity of the religious life of a free society confronts each of the faiths comprising that diversity. The problem succintly put is how a religion can retain its sense of theological uniqueness and yet work with other religions in the concord which can be maintained only through a recognition of equality. It may not be possible to resolve this dilemma in theory. But there is a synthesis which life rather than philosophy can effect. Joint efforts can take place without a theoretic resolution of the dilemma. Whitehead once pointed out that a contradiction may be fatal in logic and yet operate in life with creative power. As religions work side by side in the common cause of racial justice, psychological forces will be released which will not overthrow the theological doctrine of uniqueness but by a miracle of the human spirit overcome it as a barrier to cooperative enterprise. The existence of the doctrine does not weaken the mutuality which grows out of joint endeavor, participated in by men of diverse faiths. Since religion accepts responsibility for social betterment, it must realize that this responsibility can best be discharged by the pooling of the religious strength of the land. The logic of life in a free society is that theological apartness need not be accompanied by social ghettoization and untouchability.

The story is told that during World War II a Commanding Officer in receiving a new Chaplain assigned to his base, said, "Chaplain, you take charge of their souls, I'll take over every-

thing else." The Commanding Officer, it is hoped, knew more
of military organization and strategy than he did of religion,
the nature of man or of life. The rigidity of division of function
which he sought to impose on his Chaplain broke down the
first time he issued an order to his men. For it is obvious that
what he thought of the souls of men would not only determine
the way he spoke to them, but also how he would treat their
bodies. A Chaplain who, when asking of one of the G.I.'s in his
charge "how are you?" would refer only to the state of their
souls, would render himself incapable of understanding their
spiritual needs. The ways in which we earn our livelihood influence deeply the spiritual life we lead. An economy reflects
and imposes a value-system, a moral code—I almost said a
theology. I have already mentioned the ever widening scope
of governmental activity. It legislates for and supervises a far
vaster portion of our common and individual life than ever
before. It renders decisions and organizes programs which embody ethical values and principles. Social projects and policies
have moral consequences. Religion without claiming special
privilege in the arena of public and political affairs should not
on the other hand suffer a disenfranchisement in a free society
which is not demanded of any other voluntary collectivity. Religious belief does not make one less of a citizen and when believing citizens are joined in a believing body, they should not
be deprived, nor ought they deprive themselves of their inalienable rights to participate in the normal processes of discussion, political action and pressure.

Secondly, religion in the fulfillment of its own nature should
bring to bear upon the social ills and needs of our time its
unique concern, sensitivity, and experience. Here too, as in the
other relationships we have discussed, religion should wisely
practice a number of proper and necessary restraints. I have
already indicated that it should not seek preferment in any

form. It should avoid any appearance of seeking control. In favoring any type of social program, it must not expect nor should it receive, immunity from criticism and opposition which are part of the "free trade of ideas" in a democracy. It must never, in dealing with a specific issue or problem, draw its ecclesiastical robes about it and shout "Sanctuary" when it is challenged or refuted. But far and beyond all this it must not abdicate its role as a critic of the illusions, inadequacies, and errors of the political life of its times. It should not seek to impose upon a society comprising diverse faiths and viewpoints, laws which mirror only its own specific doctrinal beliefs and principles. Its universality must come into full play even when it acts in its capacity as a particular church or religious body. Its public stance must not only derive from its general religious orientation but also from the study and knowledge of contemporary life and of the particular issue on which it expresses itself in word and action. I can visualize no type of customary and legitimate action in the sphere of political life which is to be denied to organized religion short of promoting the candidacy of a particular candidate. Its responsibility is to ideas and ideals; to the humanization of our technological society, to the enhancement of human welfare and to those principles of justice and truth which government no less than other agencies should seek to embody and advance.

There are no limits to the sacrifice and devotion which those whose ultimate loyalty is to God can attain. When religion draws upon its own deepest resources, it will not stop in its pursuit of the right even when its prestige, safety, institutions or its very life are endangered. It can have no vested interest in its struggle for justice other than in the truths it affirms and the purposes to which it is dedicated. It will be awed neither by majority opinion, governmental power, or the resignation of many of its own adherents. It will speak out though the voices of others have been muted, and will act when fear has paralyzed university, press, and every other secular agency. It will not hesitate to stand alone midst torrents of enmity and scorn. That religion can act in this heroic manner in the midst of the greatest peril and the darkest crisis is evidenced by the testimony of one who himself was not a faithful communicant. Albert Einstein wrote these words—"Only the Church stood squarely across the path of Hitler's campaign for suppressing the truth. I feel a great affection and admiration because the Church has had the courage and persistence to stand for intellectual truth and moral freedom. I am forced to confess that what I once despised, I now praise unreservedly."

No preachment or doctrinal exposition will as fully reveal to our time the scope and power of religion as this capacity for independence and commitment in the midst of contingencies and relativities, which no other phase of life can in equal measure manifest. To fulfill this singular potentiality is both the responsibility and privilege of religion.

PART V

....

Perspectives on the Challenge

Interracial Justice and Love: Challenge to a Religious America

ALBERT CARDINAL MEYER
J. IRWIN MILLER

DR. JULIUS MARK

Senior Rabbi of Temple Emanu-El, New York City
President of the Synagogue Council of America

The great religious communions of our country—Catholic, Protestant and Jewish—have affirmed on many occasions their conviction that all men are created in the image of God and are equally regarded as His children by our Heavenly Father. They have expressed their abhorrence of every form of prejudice and bigotry on the grounds of differences in racial background. They have vigorously condemned as evil and unjust discrimination in employment, housing, schooling, transportation and the use of public facilities which have been established to serve the entire community.

Now the three major religious bodies of our country have come together to speak out with one voice, in the name of the one God Whom we all worship, in an effort to impress not only our own congregants but the entire American people with the urgent necessity of translating into daily practice the noble concepts of human equality which we have many times individually proclaimed.

The equality of all men is a basic principle of the American way of life. The Declaration of Independence proclaims that "all men are created equal" and "are endowed by their Creator with certain unalienable rights, that among these are Life, Liberty and the Pursuit of Happiness." The Emancipation Proclamation, issued by the immortal Abraham Lincoln a century ago on the first of this month, outlaws human slavery and the famed Supreme Court decision of 1954 declares unconstitutional the practice of segregation of the races in schools maintained by the people.

Laws enacted by legislative assemblies are, to be sure, important. Their mere passage, however, is not enough. The widespread resistance to these man-made laws in the North as well as the South—we must not forget that our problem is not sectional, but national—is a challenge to all of us who believe in God's Fatherhood and man's brotherhood to stress and proclaim anew the higher, God-made laws proclaiming the precious worth of every human being and at the same time to humbly confess our failure to implement them in our own lives.

It appears to me that if we are to make a meaningful and concrete contribution to the resolution of the shameful and humiliating condition known by the evil word "racism," we must first have a clearer concept of the relation of religion to the social, political, educational and economic problems of life. Is religion a way of looking at *certain things* or is it a *certain* way of looking at *all* things? To some, religion either by definition or by the way they react to life's problems, is a way of looking at certain things. To them religion's sole or principal function is to be concerned with such matters as God, church attendance, retreats, ceremonials, observance of Holy Days and festivals, immortality, sin, repentance, and so forth. They maintain that areas and problems such as business, industry, race relations, slums, poverty, child labor, social security, social justice, civil rights, segregation are all outside the purview of religion. To them religion has no relevance to everyday living. They would agree with the 19th century statesman who remarked: "Things have come to a pretty pass if religion is going to interfere with private life." They lustily sing "God is in His Holy Temple" and then make sure that He remains within the confines of the sanctuary instead of taking Him with them into the highways and byways of everyday living.

There are others, however, who insist that while prayer, ritual and ceremony play an important role in religious living, these by no means constitute the totality of religion. To them, religion in its truest and finest sense is a *certain way*, based upon man's awareness of God and God's requirements of His children, of looking at *all* things. For them religion is only partly concerned with enabling souls to enter heaven. Its principal purpose is to help create a little more heaven on earth for all the children of God as taught by the prophets of the Bible. That is why the prophets preached against corrupt politics, land monopoly, social injustice, racial bigotry, national arrogance. Micah summed up his concept of religion in the famed utterance wherein he declared that walking humbly with God constitutes just one-third of our Heavenly Father's requirements of man. The other two-thirds consist of doing justly and loving mercy.

It is, of course, one thing to proclaim lofty teachings which envisage a society wherein all human beings live together as brothers. It is quite something else to implement these principles of simple justice. When a priest, minister or rabbi exercises his right, as a teacher of religion, to denounce not alone evil but evil-doers and speaks out forthrightly in defense of those who are denied the elementary rights which belong to all human beings, he is likely to share the experience of Amos, who was told in so many words by Amaziah, the priest of Beth-El: "Go peddle your radicalism somewhere else, where the overhead isn't so high."

In the minds of many laymen—and some ministers of religion—there appears to be a dichotomy between religion and life. They insist that preachers confine themselves to purely "religious" matters, which have little or nothing to do with the practical affairs of life. Several years ago a young rabbi expressed both amusement and sadness when he learned that an important member of his congregation vigorously objected to a passage in one of his sermons wherein he expressed sympathy for a young Negro who had been brutally murdered by a mob. His congregant objected on the grounds that his rabbi "had no business mentioning politics" in his sermon. The pulpit of this rabbi, by the way, is not in Mississippi or in some other Southern communty, but in enlightened California. Basically, race prejudice is not a political or an economic problem but a moral and religious problem.

We must make it crystal clear that while we are all uncompromisingly loyal to our respective religious convictions, practices and ceremonials, we are united as sons and daughters of Catholicism, Protestantism and Judaism in our equally uncompromising affirmation that God "hath made of one blood all nations of men for to dwell on all the face of the earth" (Acts 17:26), and that all human beings are descended from one common ancestor, proving thereby that no man is racially superior or inferior to his fellowman. Created in the image of the Divine, all men enjoy equal spiritual dignity. They are entitled to the same rights and upon all alike devolve the same responsibilities.

It is well known that proponents of racism and segregation have quoted the Bible to prove the existence of superior and inferior races as a manifestation of God's will. Thus, shortly before the outbreak of the Civil War a distinguished rabbi of New York City, Morris J. Raphall, delivered a scholarly address which brought comfort to believers in human slavery. Rabbi Raphall was only one of numerous ministers of religion throughout the centuries and even to our day who pointed to many biblical ordinances and laws as evidence that the Bible condones slavery. That the Bible also condones polygamy seemed to have escaped their notice. The fact is that a great many customs and practices to be found in the Bible merely reflect the mores of ancient society. Rabbi Raphall's far more scholarly contemporary, Rabbi David Einhorn, then of Baltimore, was forced to flee from his city when a mob threatened him with lynching after he had called slavery "the greatest possible crime against God."

The fact is that the Bible, while recognizing slavery, constantly tries to humanize the institution. Thus, while as late as 1854 the Congress of the United States passed a law making it mandatory to restore fugitive slaves to their master, the book of Deuteronomy (23:16-17) commands

> Thou shalt not deliver unto his master a slave that is escaped from his master. He shall dwell with thee . . . in the place which he shall choose within one of thy gates, where it liketh him best; thou shalt not wrong him.

Even more significant is the experience of Miriam, sister of Moses, as recounted in the book of Numbers (12:1-9), when she and Aaron "spoke against Moses because of the Ethiopian woman whom he had married." She is punished by being stricken with leprosy. Aaron pleads with Moses that she be forgiven. Moses prays to God on her behalf and after seven days she is healed.

Like all peoples, ancient and modern alike, the Hebrews of Biblical times regarded themselves as the chosen of God. As proof of their superiority, they would point to their miraculous deliverances from Egypt by God's mighty hand an outstretched arm. The prophet Amos reminds his people that all races and peoples are equally loved by God when he cries: "Are ye not as the Ethiopians unto Me, O children of Israel? saith the Lord" (9:7). Yes, God brought Israel out of Egypt, but he also brought the Philistines out of Caphtor and the Syrians out of Kir.

The glorious and undying message of the book of Jonah is oft obscured in the minds of many by reason of the unimportant and inconsequential incident of the whale or, as the story has it, the "great fish" which God had especially prepared. Jonah is commanded by God to journey to Nineveh, "that great city," and plead with the people to mend their ways lest they be destroyed by the corruption and wickedness into which they had fallen. The prophet flatly refuses to obey God's command, boards a ship and begins his journey westward toward Tarshish rather than eastward in the direction of Nineveh. Why? Because he feels himself superior to the people of Nineveh, has no pity for them and is quite content for them to be destroyed. Whereupon God again orders him to go to Nineveh and this time he obeys. He preaches to the people and *mirabile dictu*, they hearken to him, repent and are saved from destruction.

Now one might think that the prophet would have rejoiced over his successful preaching mission. But not Jonah! He is exceedingly displeased and downright angry over the outcome, even to the point of wishing that he were dead. Then he is again filled with anger when a gourd which God had caused to grow out of the earth to shield him from the sun withers the next morning. The sublime lesson of God's concern for all His children, whatever be their race or creed or nationality, is driven home in the last two sentences of the book of Jonah.

And the Lord said: "Thou hast had pity on the gourd, for which thou hast not labored, neither madest it grow, which came up in a night and perished in a night; shouldst thou not have pity on Nineveh, that great city, wherein are more than six score thousand persons that cannot discern between their right hand and their left hand, and also much cattle?

In view of its significant and enduring challenge to humankind throughout the ages and even to our own times, it is not surprising that the ancient Rabbis ordained that the book of Jonah should be read in all Synagogues on the Day of Atonement, the most sacred Holy Day in the Jewish religious calendar, a practice which is observed to this very day.

Racial discrimination has been defined as "the unjust separation of people from things and circumstances" and segregation as "the immoral separation of people from people" (Kyle Haselden). Many organizations are dedicated to breaking down the cruel walls and barriers which divide people from people. They demand that the right to vote, to equal educational opportunities, to equal employment opportunities and to adequate housing shall be denied to no man on account of difference in race. In this battle to build a society and a world in which the dignity of every human beings is jealousy guarded and the equality of all men taken for granted, the forces of religion, if they are true to their purpose, must, both by precept and example, be in the forefront—leading and not following, courageously fulfilling their prophetic mission of being the conscience of humankind.

ALBERT CARDINAL MEYER
Archbishop of Chicago

At the 100th anniversary of the Emancipation Proclamation we find ourselves seized with the nation's unfinished business. We have not yet completely bridged a deep cleft that two centuries of slave economy have inflicted upon our society. The deepest cleft, the distance between master and slave, was not just the distance between the rich and the poor, between the civilized and uncivilized, the learned and the unlearned, the fortunate and the unfortunate. The gulf that separated master and slave under the regime abolished by President Lincoln's proclamation was none other than the difference between human personality, with all its rights and privileges, and the condition of a being—human in appearance, form, emotion and spiritual capacities—but totally deprived of any inherent rights, or dignities save those which were gratuitously accorded to him by his master.

It was the difference between a human being, however poor, however degraded, and that of a mere chattel. In many cases this being was honored, even loved, yet he remained stripped of those elementary rights which are the mark of our humanity itself.

The history of Negro people in the United States in the hundred years that have elapsed between the Emancipation Proclamation and the present day is one of gradually and painfully shaking off persistent remnants of those shackles with which they were once shamefully bound. Great progress has been made. There exists today not a single vocation or profession in the United States in which some men and women of the Negro people are not found. Yet despite all progress, the process of liberation remains partially unfulfilled.

We do not need to travel to any particular part of our country in order to verify the truth of the last assertion. We need only look at the racial problems which confront us in the cities of our Northeast, of the Great Lakes, and of the Far Western regions, to realize the extent of the work that still confronts us. The unresolved race question is indeed a pathological infection in our social and political economy. It is also an obstacle to a right conscience before God. Our whole future as a nation and as a religious people may be determined by what we do about the race problem in the next few years. Careful and responsible thinkers refer to racism as the core of many of our problems today. What we do about it is the ultimate test of our vaunted democratic way of life. More than this, however, it is the ultimate test of our understanding of Christianity, as expressed in the words of the Divine Master: "By this will all men know that you are my disciples, if you have love for one another" (John 13:35).

This unfinished business, therefore, is the gravest kind of challenge to all who believe in a loving Creator, to all who honor His revelation through the ages, to all who feel a deep moral concern for the human person whose integrity He has committed to the conscience of the struggling human race. How can any of us claim to possess a deep love of the human family, and yet be unconcerned about prevailing racial attitudes that directly militate against the family, and against its very existence as a basic institution of our human society?

Nothing is more foolish or illogical than to take the difficulty or complexity of our unfinished business as an excuse for inaction. To take this attitude, would be, indeed, to tempt the Lord. Our Heavenly Father Himself, so familiar with our inconsistencies and weaknesses, must wonder when He sees the almost infinite skill, resourcefulness and delicacy of operation by which our astronauts succeed in launching and guiding tiny capsules through boundless space; yet apparently we are unable to banish prejudice and gross ignorance and cruel racial injustice from our communities.

On the contrary, the presence and the complexity of our difficulties are a call to action, to concrete and determined action. No action, however, can be divorced from the principles which inspire it. Indeed, in the words of the late Pope Pius XII: "There are occasions and times in which only recourse to higher principles can establish clearly the boundaries between right and wrong, between what is lawful and immoral, and bring peace to consciences faced with grave decisions." Let us, then, frankly acknowledge that we are dealing here with a moral and religious issue, as the Catholic Bishops of the United States said in their statement of 1958: "The heart of the race question is moral and religious."

The Holy Bible, though it centers in the record of God's call to man and man's response to God, sheds a guiding light on the investigation of man's action in human society and on the principles which must govern all men in their human dealings with one another. Sacred Scripture, therefore, sheds white light on the principles of human relations. Men are equal in God's plan and all can participate in the fulness of His blessings. Human nature is to be fulfilled divinely in membership in God's own family. This plan of God, as described in the Scriptures, is the gratuitous fulfillment of man. In it all men are called to an exalted, divine dignity, and all men are equally impotent to fulfill themselves. God fulfills man, and men are to be united in charity as brothers in the family of God. In this light man's nature contains a potency for equality on the divine level, which consecrates a natural right to equality on the human level. For the Christian, both in the Old and the New Covenants, God has envisioned the unity and equality of all men in His plan of salvation.

I shall not attempt here to spell out the biblical passages which illustrate this statement. Suffice it to say that we are committed to the proposition that all men are equal in the sight of God; that is, they are created by God, and in the faith of Christian life, they are redeemed by His Divine Son; they are ennobled by the Law of God, and God desires them as His friends in the eternity of heaven. This fact confers upon all men human dignity and human rights. Men are unequal in talent and achievement; they differ in culture and personal characteristics. Some are saintly, some seem to be evil, most are men of good will, though beset with human frailty. On the basis of personal differences we may distinguish among our fellow-men, remembering always the admonition: "Let him who is without sin cast the first stone." But discrimination based on the accidental fact of race or color, regardless of personal qualities or achievement, is as such injurious to human rights and cannot be reconciled with the truth that God has created all men with equal rights and equal dignity.

It is easy to proclaim moral issues, but experience teaches us that mistaken or misguided attempts to deal with such issues can land us ultimately in a situation precisely the opposite of that first intended.

Marxism and communism presented themselves originally as attempts to deal with grave moral problems that were raised

by a glaring inequality between the rich and the poor in a growing nineteenth-century industrial civilization: by the grievous
abuses created by the wealthy, powerful man's exploitation of
the workingman and his toil, by shamefully inadequate wages,
by wretched living conditions, and, in short, by the situation
presented in a new type of master and slave. Yet the measures
proposed resulted not in greater freedom for the individual or
society but in the most brutal and absolute tyranny the human
race has ever seen.

So, too, in the field of interracial relations, White Citizens'
Councils, Black Muslims movements, and all such separatist
efforts lead not to man discovering his own true nobility, not to
man raising his head in equality, but rather to man raising his
fist in inequality, in terror, in demoralizing antagonism.

But the business of religious leaders is not that of registering
merely some kind of instinctive reaction against the grave dis-
orders and injustices, the social and racial antagonisms that are
growing up in our communities. Nor is it the business of merely
uttering some kind of an eloquent protest, valuable as such a
protest may be. Our great work is to lay the foundation for that
kind of reaction which will achieve lasting benefits. It is the
kind of action called for by Pope John XXIII in his memorable
encyclical letter, *Mater et Magistra*, when he wrote: "It is not
enough merely to publicize a social doctrine; it has to be trans-
lated into action. This is particularly true of Christian social
doctrine, whose light is truth, whose objective is justice, and
whose driving force is love." What is needed is the kind of
action which takes into account the whole nature of man, the
demands of his personality, and the necessary integrity of his
social institutions, and is determined to spare no effort that
this personality and these institutions may be honored. Our
homes, our hospitals, our professional organizations and practices, our schools and colleges, our real estate operations, our

police protection, in short all forms of public association and activity are involved.

For this reason I point out now two massive questions which face us, and certain types of action which seem to me to be the most effective in order to handle them. The two particularly urgent, massive questions that face all who attempt to foresee the future of our large city communities are: first, the future of our urban youth in the matter of employment and training for useful, honorable careers, and, secondly, the vexed question of residential segregation, with all its implications in the field of home life, family morals, and community peace and friendship.

We observe today an ever growing number of minority group youth who are dropping out of school at an alarming rate. In which direction are these young people headed? Are they to swell the ranks of those who congregate upon our street corners and are merged into the nameless mass of the disaffected, discouraged, and criminal? Are they to be the ready victims of the narcotics peddler?

Or are they to avail themselves of an ever growing demand for talent, in the field of technological employment? Are their talents to be salvaged, as the current phrase goes?

Is there more that we can do to end unfair job discrimination based on race, religion, national origin? Have we done all that we could even within our own institutions to open up employment opportunities to qualified minority group personnel, to go out of our way to create incentive for those who need it most, and thus build up in youth a desire for learning and technical skills?

Again we observe the spread of urban neighborhoods that have been abandoned by their former owners—either through fear of minority groups or various types of economic and social pressure. We see the consequent growth of the segregated Negro area, as the old neighborhoods are solidly populated by

Negroes. We know the tension, and sometimes violence, that accompanies this transition—and the difficulties of maintaining peace, law, and order in the community.

Are we to continue to see fear and panic seize the white community in areas facing racial change? Will we see homeowners continue to yield to the professional manipulators of the panic button and to the ruthless blockbusters?

Or can the force of religion be used more effectively to prepare for change, to help create community organizations which grow, not from fear, but from pride and stewardship over property, as well as from the spirit of neighborliness and openness to all who will maintain community standards? At the same time can religion help more effectively to establish the spirit and practice of open occupancy for an entire metropolitan area such as our own—because this is the only good atmosphere for our young people, white and Negro alike—and because this will relieve the pressures that generate panic, flight, and desperation?

The types of action which suggest themselves as most effective are not something startlingly new or original. Rather, they represent a brief summary of what experience has already taught in the matter of race relations and interracial cooperation, and is most likely to lead to definite results in the near future. For, we are not dealing with abstract propositions, but with living, suffering, and hoping human beings; with parents and children, with husbands and wives, with the young and the aged, with the healthy and the sick, with old-line Americans and recent immigrants.

First of all, we have to work together. The problems that now confront us in our great cities are too manifold and too deep-rooted in human passions and misunderstandings for any one of our great religious bodies to deal with them alone.

Certainly each of the many organizations represented in this conference can operate and should be expected to operate—wherever conditions permit—among those of one's own faith and spiritual allegiance. No one can honestly point to others for action if one's own record is incomplete. Nevertheless, this matter of combating racial prejudice and its bitter fruits, and of establishing a really integrated community is by its very nature a task for us all: not separately and alone, but jointly as well. To this common task each of us brings his own store of experience and wisdom.

Indeed, I think it is only fair to expect that by our joint action we shall learn better to understand one another. There is no surer way for the various religious bodies who love a common Father than to unite in studying and meeting our common responsibilities and the needs of our troubled fellow citizens.

For a similar reason a work of this kind should, it seems to me, be undertaken by the generous cooperation of all elements concerned: by the cooperation of the different racial groups quite as well as of the different faiths. A joint meeting such as that in which we are engaged would mean little if it were confined to the leaders of any one group or race. The Catholic Archdiocese of Chicago has undertaken to emphasize as fundamental this principle of racial cooperation, through its various agencies and through its Catholic Interracial Council, where intelligent and public-spirited men and women unite in frank, across-the-board discussions of the sources of racial conflicts and the best way of dealing with them.

The love of God, our heavenly Father, and the love of neighbor as a child of God cannot in action be a one-way street. Rather, love seeks a common footing and leads to joint efforts, in which mutual difficulties and obstacles are laid openly upon the table, and dealt with in a manner devoid of narrow self-interest or of timid human respect or mere political conniving.

It is difficult to exaggerate the critical nature of the present hour. I am not referring to the dangers from abroad, grievous as these are, but to the situation at home.

Are the various racial groups to waste their energies and dislocate the nation itself in a fruitless, hopeless struggle between despair on the one hand and unreasoned fear on the other? Or are we all, of every national or ethnic or racial origin, determined to work together for the good of our communities and of our nation, and for the glory of our God and Father?

The choice is ours: the responsibility of example and initiative falls upon the shoulders of our country's religious leaders.

The unfinished business of the Emancipation Proclamation demands that we remove the last vestiges of injustice, legal inequality, and discrimination from our communities, our parishes, our schools and other public institutions. We shall not relax in that task until the work is completed, and the stain of racial inequality removed from our nation and our cities.

But we can speak of unfinished business in a much deeper and wider sense, which is that of setting free the constructive, creative power of the Negro people of the country. It is a question not merely of avoiding and banishing racial injustices. Our goal is a much higher one: to set free, for the glory of God, as well as for the good of our nation and of the world, the gifts, the talents—as yet hardly plumbed—spiritual and cultural of all sections of our human community. Only God our Lord knows what spiritual forces are waiting to be released, if we have but the faith and the love to do. The coming of inmigrant or immigrant racial groups to our local communities often poses problems, but the problems are not agonizing and overwhelming if the newcomers are our brothers. The newcomers bear gifts, if we have the intelligence and the imagination to help them develop them.

As you are well aware, it is my privilege to take part in the world-wide Second Vatican Ecumenical Council, that is meeting in Rome. The "Message to Humanity" with which this Council opened its first session last October, seems to me peculiarly appropriate for the very task in which we have jointly engaged.

"In the performance of our earthly mission," said the Fathers of the Council on that occasion, "we take into account all that which pertains to the dignity of man and all that contributes toward the real brotherhood of nations." The conciliar assembly alluded to its own "admirable diversity of races, nations and tongues," and urged every effort "to unite all peoples and to create among them a mutual esteem of sentiment and of works."

"We proclaim," said the assembled bishops, "that all men are brothers, irrespective of the race or nation to which they belong."

But, following the principles of Pope John, they were not satisfied with mere high-sounding declarations. They urged all conscientious men and women to work for social justice, and declared that "the Church is today absolutely necessary to the world, to denounce injustice and shameful inequalities, to restore the true order of goods and things so that, according to the principles of the Gospel, the life of man may become truly human."

"Therefore," said the Council, "we humbly invite all to collaborate with us to establish in the world a more ordered way of living and greater brotherhood. We invite all, not only our brothers of whom we are the pastors, but all our brothers who believe in Christ and all men of good will whom God wishes to have saved and led toward the knowledge of the truth.

"It is in fact the Divine will that the kingdom of God, through means of charity, shine even now, in certain sense, upon the earth, almost in anticipation of the eternal kingdom."

These words are inspired by a great hope. They are a reflection of the religious-motivated optimism of the beloved Pope John XXIII, who after describing the virtues of St. Martin de Porres, recently declared a saint, concluded with this ardent wish: "May the light of his life illumine all to walk in the way of Christian social justice and universal charity without distinction of color or race."

The words of the Council Fathers are not only words of hope. They are a challenge to our love and sense of justice, a call to heroic painstaking effort on the part of all people of good will. The evil spectre of racial hatred in our midst cannot be banished by mere high-sounding words. It cannot be banished by court action. It cannot be banished even by the application of legal justice or the exercise of the virtue of justice alone. It can only be conquered by love—true, genuine love of God and love of neighbor. This is the supreme commandment written in large letters in the Law of Moses, as we read in the Book of Deuteronomy: "Hear, O Israel! The Lord is our God, the Lord alone! Therefore, you shall love the Lord, your God, with all your heart, and with all your soul, and with all your strength" (Deut. 6:5). And in Leviticus: "You shall love your neighbor as yourself. I am the Lord" (Lev. 19:18).

This is the supreme commandment in the teaching of Christ, who repeating the words of Deuteronomy and Leviticus, added: "On these two commandments depend the whole law and the prophets" (Matt. 22:39).

The evil spectre of racial hatred, I repeat, can be banished from our midst, can be conquered, only by the prolonged, patient intelligent effort to consecrate ourselves to the service of the theme of this Conference, which is: "Interracial Justice and Love"—a theme which I might paraphrase by saying: "Interracial justice *through* love" for it is love alone which truly unites. This is a joint work and a glorious work. May our common Father in Heaven bless our efforts.

J. Irwin Miller

President, National Council of the Churches of Christ

A great deal of embarrassing material is written on the subject of religion and race and not the least of it by persons like ourselves. We understand with our minds the perfectly clear truth that all humans are equally children of one God, the Father of us all, and, as such, have no business making distinctions which God Himself does not make. This really ought to be all that is necessary to say about religion and race. Having said this (which can be classed among the most obvious truths), we should easily secure general assent to it and be able to address ourselves to other and more difficult moral tangles. But it does not turn out to be this simple, and the reason that so much that we (who class ourselves as the "good guys" in this matter) say must still be labelled nonsense in that in those secret and hopefully undetected areas of our action and behavior, even we often find ourselves not practising what we preach.

Racial discrimination and injustice in our society is at this moment a highly visible evil, but in attacking it I think we do well to remember that it is only the visible projection above the surface of society of a total problem which may have the same

relation to the visible portion that the whole mass of an iceberg
bears to that small part which can be seen above the surface of
the sea.

Shall I mention portions of the invisible bulk? If I do, they
will seem "little" things to you. You will be surprised that I
note matters like these and in an important way try to con-
nect them with this great evil to which we are called to address
ourselves. Most of the portions relate to individuals. You know
the families who wonder if their daughter is marrying "beneath" her. As an employer, I notice that almost never can a
person bring himself to recommend for employment a man he
considers a better man than himself. You see persons anxiously
seeking election to a club or society, who turn out to be the
most vigorous wielders of the blackball, once they are in. As
men, we have to suppress (and not always with success) our
desire to exclude women from preserves that have been tradi-
tionally ours. As women, if you are honest, you will confess
that sometimes there is more pleasure in deciding whom *not*
to invite to a party, than whom to invite, and so on. This list
can be very long and is limited only by our capacity for honest
self-examination. There is not a person in this room who will
not somewhere score on it several times.

What is the significance of these hidden portions of ourselves? It lies I think in the recognition that the motives which
urge us to racial discrimination and injustice are constantly
working to produce great and small acts of discrimination daily
and hourly, in both our group and our individual lives.

Now why do we feel thus driven to deeds which we are em-
barrassed to admit, which we hope to conceal? Does not this
urge at its deepest level arise from the fact that every man in
some degree always feels alone and more than any other thing
dreads actually being cut off from the rest—alone? To this dread
and this fear he instinctively has a twin response? The first is

that he will not be alone if only he can persuade the group to take him in. The other is that he will be safely *in* only if he can keep others *out*.

Once when I was at sea in World War II, I found myself standing the mid-watch on a calm Pacific night with a gunnery officer who was a career man in the Navy. Discussing what he might like to do when the war ended, he said he had thought of entering civilian life. What he liked about civilian life what that a man had there more freedom of movement, of speech, of action. What made him hesitate, however, was that he didn't know whether he could stand having those who worked for him always free to talk back to him and disagree with him. He would have liked a society democratically organized from him on up, autocratically organized from him on down. He was an *egotist*. And "egotist"—in its most useful sense—describes a person who is so generally unsure of himself that he is unable to contemplate any situation except in terms of its supposed effect on himself. Every one of us knows that in this sense he too is an egotist—more at some times under some circumstances (and these are not our best moments), happily less at other times under other circumstances. It is this frightened concern about *me* which gives rise to our preoccupation with "*in*" and "*out*," and which prompts the host of petty acts of discrimination and injustice that pock-mark our lives.

Now, for a moment, let me change the subject and return to the direct theme of religion and race. It is very clear that this nation cannot continue to preach to the whole world (with a certain smug self-righteousness) the brotherhood of man and equal opportunity to every citizen in a free society, and at the same time continue to deny the fruits of that brotherhood and true opportunity wherever it is convenient and pleasing to the majority to do so. And perhaps the real danger of allowing our present state to persist lies not so much in possible loss of national prestige and world leadership as it does in the dread effects of what is truly a malignancy of spirit, a sort of national insanity comparable to that possessing the individual who allows himself to split, trying to harbor in himself side by side grossly inconsistent aims and standards of behavior.

It is clear that we cannot continue as we are. I think it is also clear that we are determined not to do so. And it is to our great credit that we as a nation have gained the moral courage to face up to this evil before it is too late. Visibly we are attacking it by means of laws, ordinances, policy changes, and program alterations, involving matters of employment, education, transportation, voting rights, opening of stores and restaurants and hotels and housing. The religious institutions of our land are generally committed to the support of every one of these goals in words and statements—and somewhat less generally committed in terms of action. An important part of the purpose of this conference is to help the churches and synagogues of America to discover and to embark upon those paths of specific program which will speed accomplishment of each of these needed changes in our law and practice.

But the purpose of my remarks, and the reason for my seeming detour at the beginning, is to caution that this undertaking —difficult and even perilous though it be—is not enough and is even not the most important part of our calling today. Another part—again often stated—is for our churches and synagogues to provide society with an invariable example of that which we preach, an example not only in their manner of welcome to new families, but in their finances, their community witness, their total involvement in society. Yet neither of these goes far enough. We can abolish every system and practice and custom and regulation which now offends, and, if we do not at the same time work with equal vigor and determination to eliminate the spirit which embraces and supports all these, then we will find that little has been accomplished and that somehow all the new regulations and programs have become themselves the new servants of the old spirit. It is to this mortal sickness of man that religion must address itself, without neglecting its programs of immediate action.

Our common tradition has warned man for centuries that a preoccupation with self, a surrender to all the fears to which the self is prey, is *suicide*—the ultimate tragedy. Our experience confirms the truth of this, for a society composed of persons concerned only for self is a jungle, with every man looking over his shoulder in fear, no man free, and possessing none of the achievements in which we take greatest pride. This is not a question of unpleasant duty or of right response to conscience. It goes far beyond that: It is simply a matter of *Life and Death*. You die to the extent that you are preoccupied with yourself; you live, and you are free to the extent that you can lose yourself in concern for others. The Old Testament said, "You shall love your neighbor as yourself." The New Testament: "The Commandments 'you shall not commit adultery, you shall not kill, you shall not steal, you shall not covet' and *any* other Commandment are summed up in this sentence, 'You shall love your neighbor as yourself.'"

The religious institutions of this country have the clearest duty to aid and to encourage each practical move and program which they feel works for good toward the removal of remaining areas of racial discrimination and injustice; to instruct and to make clear to all our people the cancerous nature of this evil and its threat to our society if it not be eliminated; to examine their own customs and practices; to make certain that no traces exist therein to nullify the example of their preaching and to give the lie to their sincerity. But all this is not enough; neither is it the most difficult portion of the role they are now called to play. They must also minister with love and understanding to those very individuals whose practices and ideas they reject and seek to destroy, finding ways which will speak to them in convincing terms, showing them that by persisting they are destroying society, but, even worse, they are most surely destroying themselves. It is not enough to win the battle in the law courts. Unless we are able also to win over the hearts and minds of those who stand on the other side, we have accomplished nothing for certain. No one stands in greater need of an effective ministry than these persons. How do the churches and synagogues minister with convincing, compelling love and concern to those whose most cherished convictions they reject and oppose? This is a question that must concern every actively religious man if we are to contribute in a solid manner to a final lasting solution.

There is another ministry too: And that is the ministry to those who bear in their lives the great burden of this evil—those discriminated against, those dealt injustice. Their cause is so right, the evil done them so manifest, the hurt so sharp that it is the greatest wonder they have not responded with hate and retaliation wherever they could. Our churches and synagogues have a ministry here, too, to comfort, but equally to make certain that, in winning a righteous struggle, those discriminated against preserve themselves from hatred, and throughout are able to see those with whom they are locked in conflict as children of the same Father, persons toward whom they must act only in love, understanding that to surrender to anything less within oneself is to lose all.

Finally, we have a ministry to the young, to each new generation. The churches and synagogues must assume a great share of blame that our problem is still with us. The laws that govern man's behavior are as inexorable as the laws of physics and mathematics. And the peril of violating the law of love of neighbor is as great and as certain as the peril of flying in an airplane whose wing design violates the laws of aerodynamics. This is true, and because generation after generation has been unconvinced, has thought it could choose those laws of God which it would obey, we have been endlessly killing ourselves in body and spirit. The task of religion to expose this great error is never ended. Each new generation must be convinced all over again, and in each succeeding age we must find new understanding, new language appropriate to new times, new ability to convince, and we must never think that the job can be done once and for all.

I wish to affirm that the problem immediately before our people is desperately urgent, and that it requires our courageous attention. But also the manner of our solutions is important. We must take care not to arrive at solutions or programs which leave beneath an apparently healed surface remaining germs of the old evil. Man being what he is, persistent in his foolish hope that he can please God by lending Him half an ear only, we must remain aware that this danger will never pass, and that the task of religion has to be undertaken all over again with each new generation and age.

As always, the task begins with you and me, who are not ourselves free from guilt, nor ever without need of rediscovering God's truth in our own lives.

America, Race and the World

R. SARGENT SHRIVER
Director, The Peace Corps

In a powerful and moving essay the Negro author, James
Baldwin, has described an incident which happened to him
only a few miles from here—at Chicago's O'Hare Airport. He
and two Negro friends—all well over 30—were refused service
in the airport lounge on the pretense they were too young.
After a long, noisy altercation, and after calling the manager,
they were finally served. During the entire affair not one of the
many white people said a word to help. When it was all over
one of the Negroes, a Korean War veteran, turned to the
young white man beside him and said, "You know, that fight
was your fight too." The young man turned to him saying "I
lost my conscience a long time ago" and turned and walked out.

The purpose of this meeting is to reawaken that conscience;
to direct the immense power of religion so as to shape the conduct and thoughts of men toward their brother in a manner
consistent with the compassion and love on which our spiritual
tradition rests.

In so doing you follow in a great tradition. From the time of
the ancient Hebrew prophet and the dispersal of the money-
changers, men of good will have taught us that social problems

142

are moral problems on a huge scale, that a religion which would struggle to remove oppression from the world of men would not be able to create the world of the spirit. This tradition, one which is also deeply imbedded in our own country's history, was never more evident then in the years preceding the proclamation of the emancipation whose centennary we celebrate now. At that time men of God, men of all faiths, men of the North and men of the South took to pulpit, to the press and to public squares to demand an end to the moral evil of slavery.

Many religious leaders who followed this path suffered for it. Many were condemned by their congregations and deprived of their positions. Churches were burned and physical violence was often the reward of those who spoke freely. But their efforts were a significant force in ending slavery and reshaping our society. And by their actions they not only helped to restore dignity and hope to millions of Americans, they immeasurably elevated and strengthened the churches which they served.

Today, a century later, we are given the same great opportunity. Today again, the problem of racial wrongs and racial hatred is the central moral problem of our republic. Today again, hostility and misunderstanding, and even violence, awaits the man who attempts to translate the meaning of God's love into the acts and thoughts of man. Today again, the hope for happiness of millions of Negro Americans can be profoundly affected by your efforts. And today again, religion has one of the rare historical opportunities to renew its own purpose, enhance the dignity of its social role, and strengthen its institutions and its heritage by pitting itself against vast and powerful social forces which deny the role of God in the affairs of man. It is, of course, difficult for me to speak of these matters to an audience of scholars and teachers.

I am not a theologian.

I am not an "expert" in race relations.

My only credentials are my experience here in Chicago with the Interracial Council, my work with the Peace Corps, and a layman's strong interest in making faith personally meaningful in a disturbing world.

As an official of the government I am encouraged by a meeting like this. Justice for men is a common objective of religion and government and the exclusive domain of neither.

I hope the traditional American regard for the separation of church and state will never be interpreted as an excuse for either to preempt—or ignore—the vigorous pursuit of human dignity and freedom which are the legitimate concerns of both church *and* state.

But laws and government are at best coarse and inefficient instruments for remolding social institutions or illuminating the dark places of the human heart. They can deal only with the broadest and most obvious problems: guarding against segregation in schools but not against the thousands of incidents of discrimination and hatred which give the lie to what is learned in the schoolroom. They can proclaim sweeping mandates, but the process of their enforcement is so ponderous that it takes the entire energies of the nation to secure entrance of a single Negro into an unwilling white university while thousands more are without hope of entering.

They can call for the highest standards of moral conduct, but those standards are only tortuously and imperceptibly imposed upon a community which does not accept them, verifying the dictate of Walter Raushenbush that "laws do not create moral conviction, they merely recognize and enforce them."

For even though law can compel and perhaps even educate, in the last analysis, the rule of law depends upon a legal order which embodies the convictions, decisions and judgments of the men it governs.

If we recognize that laws alone are inadequate, that legislatures and presidents cannot impose moral convictions, then we must look to those institutions whose task it is to teach moral values, to restate eternal principles in terms of today's conflicts, and to conform the daily conduct of men to the guiding values of justice, of love and of compassion. Pre-eminent among those institutions is religion and the church.

Henry Ward Beecher once wrote, "That man is not a shepherd of his flocks who fails to teach the flock how to apply moral trust to every phase of ordinary practical duty." This is one of the great lessons of the history of religion. It is a lesson of scriptures and tradition. And it is also a lesson taught by Abraham, Moses and Christ.

I find it alarming, therefore, when the government looks to religious community for its share of the task and encounters, too often, a bland philosophy of laissez-faire.

As a layman, for example, I wonder why I can go to church fifty-two times a year and not hear one sermon on the practical problems of race relations? I wonder why a conference like this does not lead to a continuing exchange of views and ideas and to a coordination of efforts to solve specific problems throughout the year. I wonder, furthermore, why each minister, rabbi, and priest does not map a specific program for his congregation—a program which will produce concrete gains over the next twelve months. Such a program could do many things.

It could bring to an end segregation in those churches and church schools where it exists.

It could include a pledge to double the number of Negro families in the congregation where Negroes now attend.

It could include the establishment of interracial councils where none exists.

It could introduce Negroes to every social and community event which the church sponsors or participates in.

It could train lay Negro teachers and leaders to participate fully in congregational affairs.

If such a program intended finally to bury religious laissez-faire in racial problems where instituted, it would encourage each member of the congregation to pledge a *tithe of his time* to removing racial barriers at work, at play, and at worship.

I wonder why an appeal requesting every church member to give a tithe of his time has not been made already. Just a few Sundays ago a Catholic weekly newspaper, *The Sunday Visitor*, devoted the whole front page to this subject of tithing, but the discussion was focused primarily on the financial aspect. George Romney, the new Republican governor of Michigan, impressed me with his recent statement acknowledging quite openly that he was accustomed to giving a tithe of his income to the Mormon church. But isn't it easier to give a tithe of your money than to give a tithe of your time? Isn't the time when you give yourself more important than the money?

Let me be more specific. The Peace Corps has shown what Americans will do when they are challenged by a high purpose. They respond enthusiastically no matter what the personal cost.

Thousands of them volunteered to serve, even in the days when the sceptics and cynics were ridiculing the Peace Corps as "a children's crusade," "a beatniks' boondoggle," and a "Kiddy Korps."

They deliberately chose a hard—and to some an unpopular— course because first, it is voluntary; second, it demands their utmost; third, it is worthwhile.

These volunteers have already written the moral to a story that is still being told. That moral: "A nation cannot require too much of its citizens if the cause is right."

Do our churches expect too little of their members in solving race problems?

Suppose 5,000 congregations in America were to set up volunteer groups to combat racial prejudice and eliminate racial tensions in 5,000 religious precincts throughout America. And suppose 5,000 were to become 10,000 or 20,000?

In thousands of communities religiously inspired volunteers would be inviting Negro families to personal social functions.

They would be organizing and joining interracial councils, securing entrance of Negroes into previously all white neighborhoods, insuring enforcement of constitutional rights to equal opportunity, and improving living conditions in segregated neighborhoods.

A profound new force would be at work in America, emanating from the deepest wells of religious inspiration and reaching for the noblest summits of human experience. That combination would be invincible.

There will be those who scoff at so pointed an effort by organized religion to deal with the major social disorder.

Some will cry "Busybodies," but they will not be the first. When a group of English bishops tried to mediate the bitter British coal strike of 1926, Prime Minister Baldwin retorted by asking how they would like it if he referred the revision of the Athanasian Creed to the Iron and Steel Federation.

Some critics will want to ignore the church's word on the thesis that it is irrelevant—like the corporation president who said, "Of course, segregation is wrong from the Christian point of view. Let's not discuss it from that point of view."

Still others will argue: "So what? Go ahead. You won't be any good but you won't do any harm either."

Few people read much history, as William Temple reminded us, otherwise they would know that history abounds with dramatic examples of the impact made by the spirit of religion upon the life of mankind.

The abolition of the slave trade, for example, was carried

through by Wilberforce and his friends in the inspiration of their Christian faith. Other faiths can point to similar accomplishments.

More recently, efforts by churches and synagogues have illustrated what can be accomplished. After his school system was desegregated, one Kentucky superintendent said, "I believe ministers and lay church leaders made the greatest contribution in getting the general public to accept desegregation."

You may be familiar with the inspiring experience in Saint Louis. The 600-member Church Federation set aside a Sunday for thanksgiving prayer for public school desegregation. It challenged pastors and members to take an open stand for integration. The Cardinal called in a general letter for all Catholic pastors to influence their hundreds of thousands of parishoners to cooperate. The Rabbinical Association urged all citizens to work and pray for its success.

On the other end, we know what can happen when religious leadership is absent. Remember Clinton, Tennessee? Ugly violence flared there when desegregation was attempted. It took 650 National Guardsmen and 39 state highway troopers led by a burly 290-pound commander to restore order after days of tension.

When a special report was written to analyze what had happened in Clinton this significant sentence appeared: "Churches were not utilized to any extent in Clinton, Tennessee."

During the crisis a Baptist minister escorted Negro students through the howling crowds. He was beaten by the mob but his courage was unshaken. What might have happened at Clinton had the religious community rallied to support him?

One man is not enough.

There must be others.

I said earlier there is no reliable justice without the machinery of justice: the Government. But the machinery of justice cannot be effective without men and women who have the will and character to make it work.

There is where we come again to religion. What is it that produces men and women with the will and character to make the machinery of justice work if it is not religious faith?

The maxim is true that politics is the art of the possible. The constant challenge we face in politics is to enlarge the area of the possible—"to lengthen the stakes" in biblical language.

But to do that requires that men change their objectives. But they can't change their objectives unless they change their prejudices and that requires changes in men's attitudes, and that requires changes in men's minds, and that requires changes in men's hearts—that the human heart is the business of religion.

So I ask: "Is there any way of creating a social order of justice if religion does not do its work in the minds and hearts of men?"

I don't think so.

Is there any way of winning racial equality if religion does not permeate its adherents with its urgent sense of personal responsibility for the injustice of our present system?

I cannot stress this too much. We believe the success of the Peace Corps is due to the fact that thousands of Americans are willing to take personal responsibility for bringing peace to the world.

They have seen their task and have set forth to do it.

In race relations there is a strong tendency to blame "society" for our errors. We pass the blame on to any one of a number of impersonal causes—environment, education, etc. Shakespeare was right: "This is the excellent sophistry of the world, that when we are sick in fortune, often in surfeit of our own behavior, we make guilty of all disasters the sun, the moon, and the stars, as if we are fools by heavenly compulsion,

knaves, thieves and teachers by spherical predominance." But
he was also right when he went on to say: "The fault, Dear
Brutus, is not in our stars, but in ourselves." It is the province
of religion to instill a sense of personal responsibility into
mankind: "If you want to cleanse the stream," so the old
proverb goes, "get at the source"—the attitudes and concepts, the prejudice and hate which pollute the stream of
political life. Government can deal with their symptoms, religion must deal with their source. I think that this is what
the Presbyterian General Assembly had in mind a hundred
years ago when it declared: "The sphere of the church is wider
and more searching than the sphere of the magistrate." Religion reaches into the sanctuary of human experience where
attitudes are formed.

We can agree government has its business, religion has its.

The important thing is to get on with the job. We have
tried in the Peace Corps to try to deal positively with the
problem. For example, we set out deliberately to recruit as
many representatives of minority groups as possible for jobs
in every echelon. We knew that members of these groups
would not ordinarily seek out these jobs, so we decided to seek
them out. Today 7.4 per cent of our higher echelon positions
are filled by Negroes. Other government agencies employ .8 per
cent Negroes in similar grades. 24 per cent of our other positions are filled by Negroes. The figure for other agencies is
five and a half per cent.

We made another breakthrough. In the beginning we were
told that the Peace Corps would never get invited to the
Muslim countries because our policies require that our volunteers be recruited without discrimination, that they be assigned
without discrimination and that they be received without discrimination.

The truth of the matter is the Peace Corps is operating in
three Muslim countries. Some of our volunteers are Jewish and

I am proud to report that every one of them has been well received by their Muslim hosts.

When I told this to high officials of the government of Israel, they found it almost impossible to believe that Jewish volunteers had received a hospitable welcome from Muslim hosts.

We sent a Chinese-American doctor to Ghana. When he rose to speak to his students they could not believe he was from the United States—"that place across the sea where no colored man can go to school." They thought he was a Chinese Communist.

In Nepal we sent four volunteers to teach in a small college. Three of them were visited one night by a young Marxist student who had studied in Peking and who had already won a scholarship to Lumumba University in Moscow. This student had also just been elected to a place on the important "panchayat" council which runs the city government.

He came to rib the volunteers about discrimination in America. "Just a minute," they interrupted him, "we will let Carl Jorgenson talk about that." And they called for a fourth volunteer who was studying in his room. Carl Jorgenson walked in, a tall young Negro, a top graduate of Harvard, the son of a leader of the NAACP in Washington. "Sure let's talk about it," he said. And they did. The young Marxist— stunned that America would let a Negro in the Peace Corps, that a Negro could graduate from Harvard, that he would be living with three white Americans—has come back time and time again to discuss America with the volunteers.

In the first days of the Peace Corps we were told that Protestant volunteers would never be accepted in the villages of Latin America. We heard that the *campesinos* had been told that if they talked to a Peace Corps volunteer their souls would be in danger of hell.

The truth is that we have volunteers all over Latin America

—many of them Protestant young men and women—and there has not yet been one incident of discrimination.

I might add that the first two volunteers killed in service died in a plane crash in Columbia with 32 Columbians. One was a Jewish boy from Chicago. The other was a young Baptist from Missouri. They died in a Catholic country. *El Tiempo*, the principal newspaper of Bogota, editorialized, "They were the first to fulfill the Rite of Blood which united them (with Columbians) in an undissoluble tie . . . their bodies . . . have fallen with those of our fellow countrymen. The sacrifice of blood is truly consumated. Two races were forged together in this dramatic incident. That this be not in vain is the ardent hope of millions of human beings."

There is only one real explanation of our success in the field of race relations. We made a deliberate effort to change old patterns. If I have any justification to speak to this august body, it is to encourage you to make a conscious deliberate assault on racial barriers. From our experience in the Peace Corps I know those barriers are vulnerable.

Let me close with a pledge and a request.

We in government will continue our efforts. We will move with all the instruments at our command to achieve justice among men. That is our pledge to you. My request is simply this: Help us. If there is to be a social order allowing the fullest possible development of individual personality, if there is to be the widest and deepest fellowship among men of different races, we need what Maritain has called Democracy of the Person. You can bring it about.

Help us to see what is our task, inspire us with the faith that God is above us and with us and that He will help us. We will try to do what is right. Stir our consciences. Strengthen our wills. Inspire and challenge us to take our principles into the toughest walks of life and make them work.

PART VI

....

A Challenge to the Churches and Synagogues

A Challenge to the
Churches and Synagogues

Dr. Martin Luther King, Jr.

America has brought the nation and the world to an awe
inspiring threshold of the future. Through our scientific and
technological genius we have built mighty bridges to span
the seas and skyscraping buildings to kiss the skies. We have
dwarfed distance and placed time in chains. We have carved
highways through the stratosphere. Through the marvelous
advances of medical science we have been able to cure many
dread plagues and diseases, alleviate our pain, prolong our
lives, and make for greater security and physical well-being.
This is a dazzling picture of America's scientific progress.

But when we turn to the question of progress in the area of
race relations, we face one of the most shameful chapters of
the American scene. In spite of the jet like pace of our scientific and technological development, we still creep at horse and
buggy speed in human relations. We must face the melancholy
fact that one hundred years after the Emancipation Proclamation, the Negro is still dominated politically, exploited economically, and humiliated socially. Negroes, North and South,
still live in segregation, housed in unendurable slums, eat in
segregation, pray in segregation and die in segregation. How

much of our national life can be summarized in that perceptive phrase of Thoreau: "Improved means to an unimproved end." Through our scientific genius, we have made of our nation (and even the world) a neighborhood, but we have failed to employ our moral and spiritual genius to make of it a brotherhood. The problem of race and color prejudice remains America's chief moral dilemma.

This tragic dilemma presents the Church and Synagogue with a great challenge. As the chief moral guardians of the community these institutions must work with passionate determination to solve the problem of racial injustice. It has always been the responsibility of the Church and Synagogue to broaden horizons, challenge the status quo, and break the mores when necessary. They are "set over nations and over kingdoms, to root out and to pull down, to destroy and to overthrow, to build anew and to plant."

Honesty impels us to admit that religious bodies in America have not been faithful to their prophetic mission on the question of racial justice. In the midst of a nation rife with racial animosity, the Church too often has been content to mouth pious irrelevances and sanctimonious trivialities. Called to combat social evils, it has often remained silent behind the anesthetizing security of stained-glass windows. Called to lead men on the highway of brotherhood and to summon them to rise above the narrow confines of race and class, it has often been an active participant in shaping and crystallizing the patterns of the race-caste system. It has so often cast the mantle of its sanctity over the system of segregation. In some communities of the South many churches are the ready lackeys of state governments. In defiance of the Supreme Court's desegregation decisions, they allow their religious education buildings to be used for private segregated schools. Nothing so completely reveals the pathetic irrelevancy of the Church and illustrates the eclipse of its spiritual power as its failure to take a forthright stand on the question of racial justice. How often the Church has been an echo rather than a voice, a tail light behind the Supreme Court and other secular agencies, rather than a headlight guiding men progressively and decisively to higher levels of understanding.

If the Church does not recapture its prophetic zeal, it will become little more than an irrelevant social club with a thin veneer of religiosity. If the Church does not participate actively in the struggle for economic and racial justice, it will forfeit the loyalty of millions and cause men everywhere to say that it has atrophied its will.

Of course, there are always those who will argue that churches and synagogues should not get mixed up in such earthly, temporal matters as social and economic improvement. There are still all too many religious institutions following a theology which stresses the total and hopeless depravity of all mundane existence and which admonishes men to seek salvation in escape from social life and in preparation for a hereafter wherein all wrongs will be automatically righted. They make an undue dichotomy between souls and bodies, love and justice, the sacred and the secular. They end up with a religion which operates only on the vertical plane with no thrust on the horizontal. But however sincere, this view of religion is all too confined.

Certainly, otherworldly concerns have a deep and significant place in all religions. Religion, at its best, deals not only with the relations of man to his fellowmen, but with the relations of man to the universe and to ultimate reality. But a religion true to its nature must also be concerned about man's social conditions. Religion deals not only with the hereafter but also with the here. *Here*—where the precious lives of men are still sadly disfigured by poverty and hatred. *Here*—where millions of

God's children are being trampled over by the iron feet of oppression. *Here*—where millions are consigned to degradation and injustice and where the habitation of men is filled with agony and anguish. *Here*—where social evils have trapped multitudes of men in dark and murky corridors where there is no exit sign and plunged others into a dark abyss of emotional fatalism. Any religion that professes to be concerned about a future good "over yonder" and is not concerned about the present evils "over here" is a spiritually moribund religion only waiting for the day to be buried.

Now let us turn to some of the specific things that the Church and Synagogue can do to face the challenges of this day.

First, they must make it palpably clear that segregation is morally wrong and sinful. It is established on pride, hatred and falsehood. It is unbrotherly and impersonal. Two segregated souls never meet in God. Segregation denies the sacredness of human personality. Deeply rooted in our religious heritage is the conviction that every man is an heir to a legacy of dignity and worth. Our Judeo-Christian tradition refers to this inherent dignity of man in the Biblical term the *image of God. The image of God* is universally shared in equal portions by all men. There is no graded scale of essential worth. Every human being has etched in his personality the indelible stamp of the Creator. Every man must be respected because God loves him. The worth of an individual does not lie in the measure of his intellect, his racial origin, or his social position. Human worth lies in relatedness to God. An individual has value because he has value to God. Whenever this is recognized, "whiteness" and "blackness" pass away as determinants in a relationship and "son" and "brother" are substituted. Immanuel Kant said in one formulation of the Categorical Imperative that "all men must be treated as *ends* and never as mere *means*." The tragedy of segregation is that it treats men as means rather than ends, and thereby reduces them to things rather than persons. To use the words of Martin Buber, segregation substitutes an "I— it" relationship for the "I—thou" relationship.

But man is not an "it". He must be dealt with, not as an "animated tool," but as a person sacred in himself. To do otherwise is to depersonalize the potential person and desecrate what he is. So long as the Negro, or other member of any minority group, is treated as a means to an end, the image of God is abused in him and consequently and proportionately lost by those who inflict the abuse.

Segregation is also morally wrong because it deprives man of freedom, that quality which makes him man. The very character of the life of man demands freedom. In speaking of freedom I am not referring to the freedom of a thing called the will. The very phrase, freedom of the will, abstracts freedom from the person to make it an object; and an object almost by definition is not free. But freedom cannot thus be abstracted from the person, who is always subject as well as object and who himself still does the abstracting. So I am speaking of the freedom of man, the whole man, and not the freedom of a function called the will.

Neither am I implying that there are no limits to freedom. Freedom always operates within the limits of an already determined structure. Thus the mathematician is free to draw a circle, but he is not free to make a circle square. A man is free to walk through an open door, but he is not free to walk through a brick wall. A man is free to go to Chicago or New York, but he is not free to go to both cities at one and the same time. Freedom is always within destiny. It is the chosen fulfillment of our destined nature. We are always both free and destined.

With these qualifications we return to the assertion that

the essence of man is found in freedom. This is what Paul Tillich means when he affirms, "Man is man because he is free" or what Tolstoy implies when he says, "I cannot conceive of a man not being free unless he is dead."

What is freedom? It is, first, the capacity to deliberate or weigh alternatives. "Shall I be a doctor or a lawyer?" "Shall I vote for this candidate or the other candidate?" "Shall I be a Democrat, Republican, or Socialist?" "Shall I be a humanist or a theist?" Moment by moment we go through life engaged in this strange conversation with ourselves. Second, freedom expresses itself in decision. The word decision, like the word incision involves the image of cutting. Incision means to cut in, decision means to cut off. When I make a decision I cut off alternatives and make a choice. The existentialists say we must choose, that we are choosing animals, and if we do not choose, we sink into thinghood and the mass mind. A third expression of freedom is responsibility. This is the obligation of the person to respond if he is questioned about his decisions. No one else can respond for him. He alone must respond, for his acts are determined by the centered totality of his being.

From this analysis we can clearly see the blatant immorality of segregation. It is a selfishly contrived system which cuts off one's capacity to deliberate, decide and respond.

The absence of freedom imposes restraint on my deliberations as to what I shall do, where I shall live, or the kind of task I shall pursue. I am robbed of the basic quality of man-ness. When I cannot choose what I shall do or where I shall live it means in fact that someone or some system has already made these decisions for me, and I am reduced to an animal. The only resemblances I have to real life are the motor responses and functions that are akin to human-kind. I cannot adequately assume responsibility as a person because I have been made the party to a decision in which I played no part in making.

Now to be sure, this may be hyperbole to a certain extent, but only to underscore what actually happens when a man is robbed of his freedom. The very nature of his life is altered and his being cannot make the full circle of person-hood because that which is basic to the character of life itself has been diminished.

This is why segregation has wreaked havoc with the Negro. It is sometimes difficult to determine which are the deepest—the physical wounds or the psychological wounds. Only a Negro understands the social leprosy that segregation inflicts upon him. Like a nagging hound of hell, it follows his every activity, leaving him tormented by day and haunted by night. The suppressed fears and resentments, and the expressed anxieties and sensitivities make each day of life a turmoil. Every confrontation with the restrictions is another emotional battle in a never ending war. He is shackled in his waking moments to tip-toe stance, never quite knowing what to expect next. Nothing can be more diabolical than a deliberate attempt to destroy in any man his will to be a man and to withhold from him that something that constitutes his true essence.

The churches and synagogues have an opportunity and a duty to lift up their voices like a trumpet and declare unto the people the immorality of segregation. We must affirm that every human life is a reflex of divinity, and every act of injustice mars and defaces the image of God in man. The undergirding philosophy of segregation is diametrically opposed to the undergirding philosophy of our Judeo-Christian heritage and all the dialectics of the logicians cannot make them lie down together.

Another thing that the churches and synagogues can do to make the ideal of brotherhood a reality is to get to the ideational roots of racial prejudice. All race hate is based on fears,

suspicions, and misunderstandings, usually groundless. The
Church and Synagogue can do a great deal to direct the popular mind at this point. Through their channels of religious
education, they can point out the irrationality of these beliefs.
They can show that the idea of a superior or inferior race is a
myth that has been completely refuted by anthropological
evidence. They can show that Negroes are not innately inferior
in academic, health, and moral standards, and that they are
not inherently criminal. The churches and synagogues can say
to their worshippers that poverty and ignorance breed crime
whatever the racial group may be, and that it is a tortuous
logic to use the tragic results of segregation as an argument for
its continuation.

A third effort that the Church and Synagogue can make in
attempting to solve the race problem is to take the lead in
social reform. It is not enough for religious institutions to be
active in the realm of ideas; they must move out into the
arena of life and do battle for their sanctities. First, the
Church must remove the yoke of segregation from its own
body. Only by doing this can it be effective in its attack on
outside evils. Eleven o'clock on Sunday morning is still
America's most segregated hour and the Sunday school is still
the most segregated school of the week. The unpardonable sin,
thought the poet Milton, was when a man—like Lucifer—so
repeatedly says, "Evil, be thou my good," so consistently lives
a lie, that he loses the capacity to distinguish between good
and evil. America's segregated churches come dangerously
close to being in that position.

The churches and synagogues must become increasingly
active in social action outside their doors. They must take an
active stand against the injustices and indignities that the
Negro and other non-white minorities confront in housing,
education, police protection, and in city and state courts. They

must support strong civil rights legislation and exert their influence in the area of economic justice. Economic insecurity strangles the physical and cultural growth of its victims. Not only are millions deprived of formal education and proper health facilities, but our most fundamental social unit—the family—is tortured, corrupted, and weakened by economic insufficiency. There are few things more thoroughly sinful than economic injustice.

The Church and Synagogue are also challenged to instill within their worshippers the spirit of love, penitence and forgiveness as we move through this period of transition. This is necessary for both oppressor and oppressed alike. Those who have been on the oppressor end of the old order must go into the new age which is emerging with a deep sense of penitence, love and understanding. They must search their souls to be sure that they have removed every vestige of prejudice and bigotry, and that they have moved away from the deadening idea of white supremacy.

But those of us who have been on the oppressed end of the old order must be equally determined to go into the new age with love and understanding. We must also add the dimension of forgiveness, realizing that the forgiving act must always be initiated by the person who has been wronged, the victim of some great hurt, the recipient of some tortuous injustice, the absorber of some terrible act of oppression. The wrongdoer may request forgiveness. He may come to himself, and, like the prodigal Son, move up some dusty road, his heart palpitating with the desire for forgiveness. But only the injured neighbor can really pour out the warm waters of forgiveness.

This is why it is my personal conviction that the most potent instrument the Negro community can use to gain total emancipation in America is that of non-violent resistance. Violence as a way of achieving racial justice is both impractical and immoral. It is impractical because it ends up creating many more social problems than it solves. It is immoral because it seeks to annihilate the opponent rather than convert him. It destroys community and make brotherhood impossible. Non-violence makes it possible for one to rise to the noble heights of opposing vigorously the unjust system while loving the perpetrators of the system.

In speaking of love at this point, I am not referring to some affectionate emotion. It would be nonsense to urge men to love their oppressors in an affectionate sense. Love is not emotional bosh. It is not spineless sentimentality which refuses to take courageous action against evil for fear someone might be offended. Love is treating fellowmen as persons, understanding them with all their good and bad qualities, and treating them as potential saints. It is helping people with no thought of receiving anything in return. It is a willingness to go the second mile and to forgive seventy times seven in order to restore the broken community. It is facing evil with an infinite capacity to take it without flinching.

I believe that this is the type of love that must guide us through this turbulent period of transition. It will cause us to enter the new age which is emerging without the fatigue and poisonous drain of bitterness. We will not seek to rise from a position of disadvantage to one of advantage, thus subverting justice. Nor will we seek to substitute one tyranny for another. We will be imbued with the conviction that a philosophy of black supremacy is as injurious as a philosophy of white supremacy. God is not interested merely in the freedom of black men, and brown men, and yellow men; God is interested in the freedom of the whole human race—the creation of a society in which all men appreciate the dignity and worth of the individual.

I am happy to say that the non-violent movement in

America has come not from secular forces but from the heart
of the Negro church. This movement has done a great deal to
revitalize the Negro church and to give its message a relevant
and authentic ring. The great principles of love and justice
which stand at the center of the nonviolent movement are
deeply rooted in our Judeo-Christian heritage.

A final challenge that faces the churches and synagogues is
to lead men along the path of true integration, something the
law cannot do. Genuine integration will come when men are
obedient to the unenforceable. Dr. Harry Emerson Fosdick
has made an impressive distinction between enforceable and
unenforceable obligations. The former are regulated by the
codes of society and the vigorous implementation of law-
enforcement agencies. Breaking these obligations, spelled out
on thousands of pages in law books, has filled numerous
prisons. But unenforceable obligations are beyond the reach of
the laws of society. They concern inner attitudes, expressions of
compassion which law books cannot regulate and jails cannot
rectify. Such obligations are met by one's commitment to an
inner law, a law written on the heart. Man-made laws assure
justice, but a higher law produces love. No code of conduct ever
compelled a father to love his children or a husband to show
affection to his wife. The law court may force him to provide
bread for the family, but it cannot make him provide the
bread of love. A good father is obedient to the unenforceable.

In our nation today a mighty struggle is taking place. It is
a struggle to conquer the reign of an evil monster called segregation and its inseparable twin called discrimination—a monster that has wandered through this land for well-nigh one
hundred years, stripping millions of Negro people of their
sense of dignity and robbing them of their birthright of freedom.

Let us never succumb to the temptation of believing that

legislation and judicial decrees play only minor roles in solving this problem. Morality cannot be legislated, but behavior can be regulated. Judicial decrees may not change the heart, but they can restrain the heartless. The law can not make a man love me, but it can keep him from lynching me. The law cannot make an employer love an employee, but it can prevent him from refusing to hire me because of the color of my skin. The habits, if not the hearts of people, have been and are being altered everyday by legislative acts, judicial decisions, and executive orders. Let us not be misled by those who argue that segregation cannot be ended by the force of law.

But acknowledging this, we must admit that the ultimate solution to the race problem lies in the willingness of men to obey the unenforceable. Court orders and federal enforcement agencies are of inestimable value in achieving desegregation, but desegregation is only a partial, though necessary, step toward the final goal which we seek to realize, genuine inter-group and interpersonal living. Desegregation will break down the legal barriers and bring men together physically but something must touch the hearts and souls of men so that they will come together spiritually because it is natural and right. A vigorous enforcement of civil rights will bring an end to segregated public facilities which are barriers to a truly desegregated society, but it cannot bring an end to fears, prejudice, pride, and irrationality, which are the barriers to a truly integrated society. These dark and demonic responses will be removed only as men are possessed by the invisible inner law which etches on their hearts the conviction that all men are brothers and that love is mankind's most potent weapon for personal and social transformation. True integration will be achieved by men who are willingly obedient to unenforceable obligations.

Here, then, is the hard challenge and the sublime opportunity: to let God work in our hearts toward fashioning a truly great nation. If the Church and Synagogue will free themselves from the shackles of a deadening status quo, and, recovering their great historic mission, will speak and act fearlessly and insistently in terms of justice and peace, they will enkindle the imagination of mankind and fire the souls of men, imbuing them with a glowing and ardent love for truth and justice. They can transform dark yesterdays of hatred into bright tomorrows of love. Men everywhere and at all times will know that our Judeo-Christian faith transformed the jangling discords of America into a beautiful symphony of brotherhood. In a real sense this conference has been a blessing. Never before have the major faiths come together to grapple with the tragic problem of race and color prejudice. The fact that such an historic conference is being held may be indicative of a greater sensitivity to racial injustice on the part of the Church and the Synagogue. For four days now, we have dwelled in this sun-lit mountain of transfiguration. We have listened to eloquent words flowing from the lips of Christian and Jewish statesmen. We have analysed with painstaking care the broad dimensions and deep complexities of this haunting problem. And now the valley of injustice, with all of its ghettos, economic inequities and demoralized children of God, stands before us in grim, stark, and colossal dimensions. Will this conference end like all too many conferences on race? Will we end up caught in the "paralysis of analysis"? Will this conference end with a high blood pressure of words and anemia of action? Well, this is the real temptation. If our thoughtful and serious deliberations do not issue forth into thoughtful and serious action, we will have assembled here in vain and all of our words will have been as sounding brass and tinkling cymbal. There is a need for more religious leaders and laymen like the seventy-five who came to Albany, Ga., and the courageous ones who joined the Freedom Ride, to move out into the Freedom Ride, to move out into the arena of positive action and make their witness real. This will do much to save the church from what Reinhold Niebuhr has recently called the "sin of triviality."

Any discussion of the role of the Church and Synagogue in race relations must ultimately emphasize the need for prophecy. May the problem of race in America soon make hearts burn so that prophets will rise up saying, "Thus saith the Lord," and cry out as Amos did, "let justice roll down like waters, and righteousness like an everflowing stream." The prophet must remind America of the urgency of *now*. The oft-repeated cliches, "the time is not ripe," "Negroes are not culturally ready," are a stench in the nostrils of God. The time is always right to do what is right. *Now* is the time to realize the American dream. *Now* is the time to transform the bleak and desolate midnight of man's inhumanity to man into a glowing daybreak of justice and freedom. *Now* is the time to open the doors of opportunity to all of God's children. St. Augustine's words speak to us as never before: "Those that sit at rest while others take pains are tender turtles and buy their quiet with disgrace."

Honesty impels me to admit that this type of forthright stand is always costly and never altogether comfortable. It may mean walking through the valley of the shadow of suffering, losing a job, having a six-year-old daughter ask, "Daddy, why do you have to go to jail so much?" But we are gravely mistaken to think that religion protects us from the pain and agony of mortal existence. Life is not a euphoria of unalloyed comfort and untroubled ease. Christianity has always insisted that the cross we bear precedes the crown we wear. To be a Christian one must take up his cross, with all of its difficulties and agonizing and tension-packed content, and carry it until that very cross leaves its marks upon us and redeems us to that more excellent way which comes only through suffering. We as Christians and Jews face today that haunting statement of Whittaker Chambers: "At the heart of the crisis of our times lies the cold belief of millions, avowed and unavowed, that the death of religious faith is seen in nothing so much as in the fact that, in general, it has lost its power to move anyone to die for it." Every minister, priest and rabbi must continually submit himself to that test.

We must make a choice. Will we continue to bless a status quo that needs to be blasted and reassure a social order that needs to be reformed, or will we give ourselves unreservedly to God and His kingdom? Will we continue to march to the drum beat of conformity and respectability, or will we, listening to the beat of a more distant drum, move to its echoing sounds? Will we march only to the music of time, or will we, risking criticism and abuse, march only to the soul-saving music of eternity? More than ever before we are today challenged by the words of yesterday, "Be not conformed to this world: but be ye transformed by the renewing of your minds."

An Appeal to the Conscience
of the American People

We have met as members of the great Jewish and Christian faiths held by the majority of the American people, to counsel together concerning the tragic fact of racial prejudice, discrimination and segregation in our society. Coming as we do out of various religious backgrounds, each of us has more to say than can be said here. But this statement is what we as religious people are moved to say together.

I

Racism is our most serious domestic evil. We must eradicate it with all diligence and speed. For this purpose we appeal to the consciences of the American people.

This evil has deep roots; it will not be easily eradicated. While the Declaration of Independence did declare "that all men are created equal" and "are endowed by their Creator with certain unalienable rights," slavery was permitted for almost a century. Even after the Emancipation Proclamation, compulsory racial segregation and its degrading badge of racial inequality received judicial sanction until our own time.

We rejoice in such recent evidences of greater wisdom and

courage in our national life as the Supreme Court decisions against segregation and the heroic, non-violent protests of thousands of Americans. However, we mourn the fact that patterns of segregation remain entrenched everywhere—North and South, East and West. The spirit and the letter of our laws are mocked and violated.

Our primary concern is for the laws of God. We Americans of all religious faiths have been slow to recognize that racial discrimination and segregation are an insult to God, the Giver of human dignity and human rights. Even worse, we all have participated in perpetuating racial discrimination and segregation in civil, political, industrial, social, and private life. And worse still, in our houses of worship, our religious schools, hospitals, welfare institutions, and fraternal organizations we have often failed our own religious commitments. With few exceptions we have evaded the mandates and rejected the promises of the faiths we represent.

We repent our failures and ask the forgiveness of God. We ask also the forgiveness of our brothers, whose rights we have ignored and whose dignity we have offended. We call for a renewed religious conscience on this basically moral evil.

II

Our appeal to the American people is this:

SEEK a reign of justice in which voting rights and equal protection of the law will everywhere be enjoyed; public facilities and private ones serving a public purpose will be accessible to all; equal education and cultural opportunities, hiring and promotion, medical and hospital care, open occupancy in housing will be available to all.

SEEK a reign of love in which the wounds of past injustices will not be used as excuses for new ones; racial barriers will be eliminated; the stranger will be sought and welcomed; any man will be received as brother—his rights, your rights; his pain, your pain; his prison, your prison.

SEEK a reign of courage in which the people of God will make their faith their binding commitment; in which men willingly suffer for justice and love; in which churches and synagogues lead, not follow.

SEEK a reign of prayer in which God is praised and worshiped as the Lord of the universe, before Whom all racial idols fall, Who makes us one family and to Whom we are all responsible.

In making this appeal we affirm our common religious commitment to the essential dignity and equality of all men under God. We dedicate ourselves to work together to make this commitment a vital factor in our total life.

We call upon all the American people to work, to pray and to act courageously in the cause of human equality and dignity while there is still time, to eliminate racism permanently and decisively, to seize the historic opportunity the Lord has given us for healing an ancient rupture in the human family, to do this for the glory of God.

Notes on Contributors

Rabbi Morris Adler, rabbi of Congregation Shaarey Zedek, Detroit, since 1938, is the author of *Selected Passages from the Torah* and *The World of the Talmud* and a contributor to leading Jewish publications.

A graduate of the College of the City of New York, Rabbi Adler was ordained, and graduated with highest honors, from the Jewish Theological Seminary of America in 1935. He has been chairman of the Public Review Board of the UAW-CIO since its founding, is a vice-president of the Jewish Community Council, and a member of the State Cultural Commission of Michigan.

The Rev. Will D. Campbell is the author of *Race and Renewal of the Church* and executive director of the Southern Project, Department of Racial and Cultural Relations, National Council of Churches.

Born in Amite County, Mississippi, Rev. Campbell received his A.B. degree at Wake Forest College, studied sociology and psychology at Tulane University, and received his B.D. degree at Yale. He has been a race relations specialist with the National Council of Churches since 1956.

Dr. Dan W. Dodson, editor-in-chief of the *Journal of Educational Sociology*, is a professor in New York University's

School of Education and director of NYU's Center for Human Relations and Community Studies.

Dr. Dodson received his B.A. degree from McMurry College in Abilene, Texas, in 1931; his master's from Southern Methodist University in 1936; and his Ph.D. from NYU in 1941. From 1945 to 1948 he helped the Brooklyn Dodgers in their preparations to break the 90-year-old color line which kept Negro baseball players out of the Big Leagues.

The Very Rev. Msgr. John J. Egan is Director of the Archdiocesan Conservation Council of Chicago, to which position he was appointed in May of 1959 after serving for thirteen years as Director of the Cana Conference of the Chicago Archdiocese.

Monsignor Egan is a member of the Board of Directors of the National Housing Conference, and a member of the Board of Governors of the Metropolitan Chicago Housing and Planning Council. He is Chairman of the Interreligious Council on Urban Affairs of Chicago.

Professor Abraham Joshua Heschel, professor of Jewish Ethics and Mysticism at the Jewish Theological Seminary of America, is internationally known as a scholar, author, and theologian. Dr. Heschel's major work in two volumes, *Man Is Not Alone* and *God in Search of Man*, has been acclaimed for its profound and creative approach to religious philosophy.

He was born in Warsaw, the descendant of a long line of Hassidic scholars. Professor Heschel received his Ph.D. in 1933 at the University of Berlin. He returned to Warsaw, but in 1939 departed for London. There he established the Institute for Jewish Learning. He came to the United States in 1940.

The Rev. Dr. Martin Luther King., Jr., has gained national recognition for his leadership in the struggle to secure civil rights for all United States citizens. Dr. King is president of the

Southern Christian Leadership Conference and co-pastor with his father of the Ebeneezer Baptist Church in Atlanta.

He is the author of *Stride Toward Freedom* and *The Measure of Man*. Dr. King received a B.A. degree from Morehouse College, Atlanta, in 1948; a B.D. degree from Crozer Theological Seminary, Chester, Penn., in 1951; and his doctorate in systematic theology from Boston University in 1955.

Dr. Franklin H. Littell, professor of church history at Chicago Theological Seminary, has written numerous scholarly and religious articles, and written or edited nine books.

He received his B.D. from Union Theological Seminary in 1940, and his Ph.D. in 1946 from Yale. Dr. Littell is a consultant to the National Conference of Christians and Jews in the area of religion in higher education and to the Association of Coordinators of University Religious Affairs.

Rabbi Julius Mark is Senior Rabbi of one of America's leading Reform Jewish congregations, Temple Emanu-El in New York City. He is president of the Synagogue Council of America, national co-ordinating agency of all three branches of American Jewry.

For many years he has been active in the leadership of the National Conference of Christians and Jews. Dr. Mark was graduated from the University of Cincinnati and was ordained at the Hebrew Union College.

Albert, Cardinal Meyer was appointed in 1959 to the College of Cardinals, and has since been named by Pope John XXIII, to the Pontifical Commission for Biblical Studies for the Second Vatican Council. Cardinal Meyer is a former professor and rector at St. Paul's Seminary in Milwaukee, where in 1903 he was born and in 1953 was named Archbishop.

The 59-year-old prelate is widely known in Roman Catholic

educational circles as a past president general of the National Catholic Educational Association, and former Episcopal Chairman of the National Catholic Welfare Conference, Department of Education.

J. Irwin Miller was the first layman ever elected to the presidency of the National Council of Churches in 1960. He holds this office through 1963.

A noted industrialist, Mr. Miller is chairman of the board of the Cummins Engine Company, and a member of the boards of a number of other major corporations. A member of the Christian (Disciples of Christ) denomination, he makes his home in Columbus, Indiana.

R. Sargent Shriver was appointed director of the United States Peace Corps in April, 1961. During the past two years he has traveled thousands of miles on behalf of this agency of international assistance.

Mr. Shriver has years of experience in civic, social and education work. He has served as president of Chicago Board of Education and for five years as president of the Catholic Interracial Council of Chicago. Mr. Shriver is a lawyer and received both his B.A. and LL.B. degrees from Yale University.